Sometimes They Sang with Us

Sometimes They Sang with Us

Stories from Boston's Most Enduring Neighborhoods

VOLUME III
Hyde Park, Jamaica Plain,
and Mission Hill

CITY OF BOSTON   GRUB STREET, INC.

With special thanks to all of the participants
for making this book possible

OFFICE OF THE MAYOR
Thomas M. Menino, Mayor
Michael Kineavy, Chief of Policy and Planning

COMMISSION ON AFFAIRS OF THE ELDERLY,
    CITY OF BOSTON
Eliza Greenberg, Commissioner
Tula Mahl, Deputy Commissioner
Sheila Lawn, Special Assistant to the Commissioner
Eileen O'Connor, Staff Photographer

GRUB STREET, INC.
Eve Bridburg, Founder and Executive Director
Marc Foster, Board of Directors
Christopher Castellani, Artistic Director
Alexis Rizzuto, Project Manager and Series Editor,
    The Memoir Project
Michelle Seaton, Head Instructor, The Memoir
    Project
Whitney Scharer, Development Director
Sonya Larson, Program Manager
Whitney Ochoa, Outreach Coordinator
Chip Cheek, Administrative Coordinator
Kerrie Kemperman, Head Writing Coach and
    Assistant Series Editor, The Memoir Project
Jennifer De Leon, Spanish Instructor, Coach,
    and Translator
Kathleen Olesky, Coach, Translator, and
    Spanish Editor
Judah Leblang, Soul Brown, Patty Caya,
    Rhea Dunn, Carrie Normand, and Valerie
    Stephens, Writing Coaches
Aaron Devine, Intern and Spanish Translator

Julia Boyles, Copyediting, Text Design
    and Production
Mark Robinson, Cover Design
Todd Gieg, Photographer

Amy Ryan, President, Boston Public Library

Jean Sullivan and the Loring-Greenough House,
    Jamaica Plain

The Hyde Park Community Center

The Tobin Community Center, Mission Hill

Pat Bartevian

Borders Back Bay

Grub Street and the Memoir Project are
    enormously grateful to the following funders
    for their generous support: the Calderwood
    Writing Initiative, the Llewellyn Foundation,
    the Massachusetts Cultural Council, and the
    Boston Cultural Council.

Compilation copyright © 2010
City of Boston and Grub Street, Inc.

All essays and photographs used with permission

ISBN 978-0-615-38330-9

Senior citizens are the foundation on which Boston was built. The people who shared their memories and participated in the *Memoir Project* represent thousands of families who have paved the way for us all. The generation represented in this book believed in hard work and family values, and their tremendous sense of pride will forever shape the history of Boston.

I am hopeful this book will teach future generations about our great city.

I am honored to dedicate this book to Boston's seniors.

With sincere gratitude, I thank you.

Sincerely,

Thomas M. Menino
Mayor of Boston

Contents

Rolling with the Punches

Justice & Activism

A Better Life

Beams of Light

Foreword

You've heard that good things come in threes. You've also heard, "the third time's the charm." *Sometimes They Sang with Us,* the third volume of the Memoir Project anthology series, is great evidence for both of these truisms. Readers have already been charmed and moved and informed by the essays in the first two volumes — *Born Before Plastic* (2007) and *My Legacy Is Simply This* (2008) — and now Grub Street and the City of Boston are proud to offer stories from seniors in three additional neighborhoods: Mission Hill, Jamaica Plain, and Hyde Park. These short works, along with the accompanying set of full-page photographs, paint a compelling and intimate portrait of the times, places, and people that have shaped our city. It is no exaggeration to say that the authors in this volume have also authored the story of Boston.

These essays began in eight-week group workshops led by Grub Street instructors Michelle Seaton and Jennifer De Leon. The authors went on to revise their texts one-on-one with one of Grub Street's writing coaches, a team of dedicated mentors led by Kerrie Kemperman. In both the coaching and the small-group classroom, Grub Street stressed the importance of honesty in memoir; we asked the authors to revisit difficult and pleasant experiences alike; and throughout, we reminded one another of the beauty of documenting the details of one's life in order to preserve them for future generations.

The Memoir Project began in the summer of 2005 when Mayor Thomas M. Menino and Grub Street joined forces to design a free program for seniors that met the needs of both organizations. Grub Street wanted to expand its writing classes to teach underserved populations the craft of memoir, and the City of Boston wanted to provide seniors free programs that were rich in quality beyond traditional health and human services. In particular, Mayor Menino recognized a compelling need to enable older residents of the city to give voice to their thoughts and feelings by putting meaningful events from their lives on paper. Our first workshops were held in the North End, Roxbury, and South Boston; the next groups were held in Charlestown, Chinatown, East Boston, and Mattapan. The City of Boston ensured that every senior who wanted to participate in the program was able to attend the workshops and coaching sessions, and provided the logistical framework for all the meetings to occur.

Over the past five years, seniors from the ten Memoir Project neighborhoods have read their work at the Boston Public Library, the North End and South Boston Public Libraries, Borders Bookstore, on American Public Radio and Cambridge Community Television, and at various elementary, middle, and high schools across the city. The authors have also worked one-on-one with teenage writers, helping to bridge the gap between generations. Most recently, seniors from various neighborhoods have come together in new workshops and broadened their creative endeavors to include poetry, fiction, and other forms of narrative non-fiction.

All three volumes in this series serve as a fitting record of the lives of both ordinary and extraordinary Bostonians. We hope you enjoy the stories as much as we have enjoyed working with these new authors, and that their work prompts you to record your own history and unique perspective in whichever way inspires you.

CHRISTOPHER CASTELLANI
Artistic Director, Grub Street

MAYOR THOMAS M. MENINO
City of Boston

MARC FOSTER
Board of Directors, Grub Street

ELIZA GREENBERG
Commissioner on Affairs of the Elderly

Introduction

This, the third volume in the Memoir Project series, is the first to be published since our country began experiencing the current economic downturn. Not serious enough to equal the Great Depression, it has been dubbed a "recession." Whatever the title, it has tested the American people. As I read through these remarkable stories, every one speaks to me in different ways of the mettle of the generations that have come before.

Whether fighting for an education, working hard for a livelihood, or taking care of one's family after losing a spouse, the writers epitomize that great Emersonian mandate: self-reliance. Time and again, the self-reliance of families growing their own food during hard times on whatever land was available comes into play. I can't help but think of the current resurgence of home gardening, even in urban areas. This year I've dedicated my own "victory garden" to the memory of my widowed great-grandmother who fed her family with an urban farm in Malden almost a century ago.

Along with making your own way and your own food are stories of making your own fun. You'll read about children singing with friends in impromptu sidewalk concerts, engaging in neighborhood food fights, amusing themselves with an imaginary family, and attending a birthday party to which only those *with* whooping cough were invited.

The idea of self-reliance does not mean that every person is an island. It extends to families, neighborhoods, and communities, as you'll see in accounts of older family members who light the way to success for those coming after them despite obstacles of race, gender, or poverty; neighbors who extend business opportunities to friends; and communities that organize to fight for justice and equality.

One senior whose story exemplifies many of these themes is Mary Clifford (1933–2010), who struggled to hold her business together and keep her customers happy as inflation drove up prices and the neighborhood changed. She ultimately lost that battle but shares her lesson with us: while money comes and goes, it's how we treat others (our friends, families, neighbors, and strangers) that determines who we are.

Another senior we'd like to honor is Gladys Chute Facey (1922–2010), who was known as "Miss Facey" or "The Lady in Purple" to two generations of residents in Jamaica Plain's Bromley Heath Housing Complex. For more than thirty years she was the sometimes-paid, sometimes-not babysitter to the housing complex's children. The money was unimportant to Gladys; those many, many children were payment enough. After the death of her daughter, she also raised her three grandchildren. She gave all of her love and time to children and her community and thanked God for the opportunity.

The personal essays gathered in this volume offer glimpses of how generations of Americans and American immigrants survived in tough times—how they weathered change, insisted on justice, looked out for one another, and got by with integrity, honesty, and a lot of hard work. In today's economic uncertainty, these stories offer us guidance on weathering the storm.

ALEXIS RIZZUTO
Series Editor

KERRIE KEMPERMAN
Assistant Series Editor

Breadwinning

ELLIE'S COFFEE AND DONUT SHOP

Mary Clifford

The friend who changed my life was named Ellie. Everyone in school loved Ellie. She was a wonderful person, and after high school she opened a donut shop. Who knew that I was going to own it myself someday? Ellie's father, whom I called Pa, was a very tall Englishman and head baker for A&P. He taught all the bakers how to bake for their stores. Ellie was one of ten children, and as Pa had taught them all to bake, they each had their own bakery or business. One of the children in East Cambridge became a master baker who made wedding cakes. Ellie had two places, one at 1518 Tremont Street and another on Warren Street. Both were called Ellie's Coffee and Donut Shop.

Ellie suffered from heart disease. She was one of the youngest in the family and as a child, she had to lift the 100-pound bags of flour. I think that weakened her heart. She went to Brigham and Women's Hospital in 1959. Her doctor was crazy about her and thought he could get her through with treatment. I still remember the day she died: April 9, 1959, at nine in the morning. We were all in complete shock. It was the saddest day of my life. My boyfriend Gene took me to the movies that night—the drive-in—and I just looked up at the stars. I couldn't believe she was gone.

After she died, Ellie's parents took over her business. They lived in my building. Since they were getting older, I ran errands for them, and they were grateful. Ellie's mother was very overweight and had trouble getting around, so I went to the post office, and brought her groceries. I stopped by their house a lot of nights to see if they needed anything and to chat with them. They offered to sell me the business for short money, about $12,000 for the business and another building. I almost died of shock. I was working as a manager at Curtis Candy at the time. I said, "No way." Pa said, "I'll teach you everything"—and he did. He stayed with me to teach me how to run the business.

At the time, I was going with a wonderful man named Gene Colantouni. I had been going with him for about thirteen years. We were at that point where I had to marry him, but I had a chance to start a business. We didn't have words over it; I wouldn't say that. But Ellie's parents were offering me this good deal to start my own business, and it was the best thing I ever did.

Pa taught me how to make donuts, but I couldn't do that and run the business too, so he taught my brother and then my brother-in-law. My father made the muffins and people raved about them. Ellie's father taught me the business part, the accounting. He even got me an accountant. I learned how to order merchandise, but not too much—just enough to keep from running out. He had me on a trial basis, while the bank was deciding if they would give me the money. After the bank gave me a mortgage to buy the business, Ellie's parents moved out of the building, and I moved in. My sister, her husband, and their two girls moved into the apartments over the business. My apartment housed my mother, my father, my brother, and me. We had three bedrooms and a long hallway. I fixed up the apartment like new, with a brand new kitchen, dishwashers, new rugs, everything to make it easy for my parents.

I had a freezer and went down to the North End once a month to buy the best meats to put in it. My nieces and nephews would come into the donut shop after school and have ice cream for free. I had a jukebox in the place. I had about three hundred customers per day, and I knew them all. I found that certain things made more money than others. I sold my coffee for fifty cents. Donuts and muffins were a nickel. I also made sandwiches for lunch. People loved those. A hamburger cost seventy-five cents. People could buy lunch for a dollar back in the 1970s. I knew everyone in the neighborhood. They came in every day. I made so much money during that time that I paid the bank back in two years. It was a happy time. I owned that business from 1962 to 1975.

I was making good money, and I tried to help everyone. I helped my friends, by cosigning on car loans. Another time, I gave money to a man in prison. He told me he needed $2,000 to pay his lawyer to help get him out. I gave it to him, because I didn't know he was in with the gangsters. He never paid me back, so I lost that money. It was an experience. I learned not to lend money so easily. It could have been worse.

In the early seventies, business was so good that I expanded. I bought two more buildings that contained businesses, including a clothing store. That may have been my downfall. I had expenses to fix those buildings up, but I didn't know how to manage the contractors or how to run these new businesses.

In 1976, I started to have trouble. The neighborhood began to change. Long-time customers moved away and new people moved in. There was a lot of racial tension at that time. Young people who were resentful about the political climate broke many of the windows on Main Street. My windows weren't broken, as I always treated everyone with respect. Even today I have friends of all nationalities, as I believe we are all brothers and sisters. I love all people. As the neighborhood changed and inflation rose, my business declined. The price of sugar went up so many dollars a bag. It was crazy. I had to raise my prices even though I knew my customers wouldn't like it. At that time, I was fifty and my life was changing, too. I liked to get out a bit and take my sister's kids to the beach every day while my sister worked at the business.

I found out that I had some enemies. I was a very successful businesswoman, and some men didn't like this. One of the men who worked at my bank had just graduated from college. He looked over my accounts at the bank, the money I was putting in every week, and my construction loans. He wasn't nice to me at all, even in the good times. As my businesses declined, I ran out of money and couldn't support all these projects. I discovered that some of the contractors had been cheating me. I asked my lawyer what to do, if I should sell some or all of the business. He said he would look into it. Before I knew it, the bank had repossessed my primary business and the building my family and I lived in. The banker arrived at my apartment, and when my seventy-nine-year-old father answered the door, the banker said, "Get out. You don't live here anymore." I never forgave him for that.

I lost everything that year. The bank sold my business quickly at auction. I have no idea who bought it. I even lost my car because I couldn't make the payments. I had no place to live, no place to go. At the very end of the year, my mother died. I was planning to go to New York to visit family after I settled my dad in a small, subsidized apartment, but I stayed with him instead. I lived with him until he died in 1984, picking up odd jobs to support us. I worked as a taxi driver for a while, but it was hard. No one wanted to hire a woman in her fifties, but I got through.

I have a good life today. I'm not rich; I don't have any money at all. I was once a lover of money — I wanted more and more all the time. Now I don't need it. I have a good life and I'm happy. I still think of Ellie, and how good she was to me. I'm glad I had the business; it was wonderful to own something and watch it grow, to support my family, and to see my customers day after day.

KEEPING BUSY
AT THE PHARMACY

Anita Jones

I come from a family of hard-working people; maybe that's why I wanted to work, to keep from being bored. It all began when I was thirteen years old. My mother served as a pastor for twenty-eight years at the Christ's Temple Church in Providence, Rhode Island, long before anyone had ever heard of a female pastor. My father was a longshoreman. Later, in 1964, he became one of two men to first charter ILA (International Longshoremen's Association) branch #1908. It was a local union for African American longshoremen and one of the very first non-Irish locals in Massachusetts.

My mother's sister worked as a pharmacist in a drugstore near where we lived in Roxbury, and so she had to babysit me during one summer when the rest of the family was working. Her name was Juanita Williams and she was a small woman. She was the first African American woman to graduate from the Massachusetts College of Pharmacy on Longwood Avenue. In fact, my aunt was already in college when I was born in 1931.

8

The drugstore where she worked was called the Highland Pharmacy. It was small compared to stores today. My aunt ran the pharmacy inside the drugstore. People bought old-time remedies that were kept in a chest of small drawers in back of the counter, such as spirits of peppermint, camphor oil, and paregoric, which was a strong medicine—opium flavored with camphor, anise seed, and benzoic acid. Customers had to sign for it when they bought it. A brown liquid dispensed with an eyedropper, sometimes mothers would rub a drop of it on the gums of teething babies. Back then people used a lot of aspirin. There were several brands, and I re-member one customer asking my aunt which was the best brand of aspirin. Was Bayer better than the others? She replied, "They are all the same." The pharmacy sold something called Elixir of Terpin Hydrate mixed with co-deine to treat chest colds be-cause it helped people with their coughing. Aunt Juanita sold a lot of medicines that she had to mix to order. She had a chest full of little drawers from which she would choose the ingredients of the medicines she would mix. Because of her job, my aunt was a respected member of the com-munity. People would come into

My pharmacist aunt, Juanita Williams

the store and ask her advice as though they were talking to a doctor—and she loved to give advice. She would listen to their complaints and tell them what medicine they needed, if she thought they needed it. She was also fond of home remedies. She told me to drink warm ginger ale for nausea and to take vitamins. She was always pushing vitamins on customers, long before they became popular. She also advised a mixture of flour and water to cure diarrhea.

I was easily bored spending most of my time in the drugstore. My aunt tried to keep me busy helping her fill prescriptions by counting pills, and she always checked my work. When she needed something that she had ordered but was not yet in stock, she would sometimes have me go downtown to pick it up from Gilman Brothers, which was located on the corner of Shawmut Avenue and what is now called Herald Street. The building is still there, although the Gilman Brothers business is not. Even this was not enough to keep me busy. I needed more work to do.

The drugstore had a fountain for ice cream. The owner of the drugstore saw that I was bored, and he let me mix ice cream floats and sodas and scoop up sundaes and banana splits for customers. When people would buy ice cream they'd say, "Pack it down." They wanted as much as they could get for their money. They would buy half pints, pints, quarts, or individual cones. Customers could choose from six to eight containers, not the dozens of flavors they have today. We had vanilla, strawberry, chocolate, coffee, butter pecan, maple walnut, and frozen pudding ice cream that had a rum flavor mixed with raisins, cherries and other dried fruit. I hated it, but many customers ordered it specially because they were very fond of it.

The ice cream came from a company in Revere and the man who delivered it was named Mr. Lepore. He was a heavy, very friendly man, and was always pleasant.

In addition to scooping ice cream, there was plenty of cleaning to keep me busy. We washed dishes by hand in those days. In the summer, people would come in off the street and ask for a glass of water, which was free, and I would get it for them. People came in all day asking for water, and I knew that I was going to have to wash every one of those glasses myself.

The drugstore also had a couple of booths where people could sit down and eat their ice cream. When I continued to complain of boredom, my aunt's boss allowed me to wait on customers, which I enjoyed. When summer ended and I returned to school at Roxbury Memorial, he gave me an after-school job. I loved always having spending money.

In the front of the store was the cosmetics counter. You could wait on customers and use the cash register, but you had to add the prices yourself using paper and pen. We had no sales tax back then, so I didn't have to calculate that. I worked two to three hours a night and made five dollars a week.

After I graduated from high school, I applied to pharmacy school. I wasn't sure what I wanted to do, but my family suggested that I try to become a pharmacist like my aunt. It was a prestigious job, although I don't know that it paid better in those days than any other job. I sent my application to the Massachusetts College of Pharmacy, my aunt's alma mater, but I was rejected. In those days, you had to put your picture in the application and because the school had already met their quota of non-white students, they turned me down. Fortunately, I had taken a second job during high school as a nurse's aid, so I stayed on at the hospital working as an assistant in their pharmacy. I took a few classes at Suffolk University. After that I got married and raised a family. I loved to study the Bible and after graduating from Bethel Bible Institute in 1977, I continued to take more postgraduate courses at Gordon College and other accredited colleges. I was always in class, learning something new. I have a shelf stacked high with certificates from learning new things. In the church I have served as usher, trustee, and now director and treasurer.

Years later, I thought my son would be the family's second pharmacist. Raymond applied to the Massachusetts College of Pharmacy in 1970 and he was accepted. He went to the college for one year and then he went to the State Police Academy in Framingham where he became part of the first class of twelve African Americans to join the state police force in 1973. Prior to that, there had only been about two or three African Americans in the history of the state police force.

I had other jobs through the years. I worked as a bank teller, then as a mailroom supervisor at a bank that began as Dorchester Savings. After branching out into other communities, it became First American. It was one of the strongest banks in the country, but they made some bad loans and the president of the bank took his own life. Then the government came in and took over the bank, like in today's headlines. Some of the employees were in tears, but I realized I was nearing retirement age, so I went into volunteer work. I helped the community and am always looking to keep myself busy.

BREADWINNING

John Clifford

My mother was the one who held the family together. She was the breadwinner. In 1931, when my father lost his job, she put me in school and went to work as a maid at the Peter Bent Hotel, which was across from the Peter Bent Hospital, now known as Brigham and Women's Hospital. My mother worked six days a week and sometimes on Sunday.

Since I had just turned five, my mother took me to enroll at Mission Grammar School. The principal, a nun, said that I was too young to be enrolled. She told my mother to bring me back the next year, when I was six. My mother told her that my father had lost his job and she had to work at the hotel to support the family, and so I needed to enroll at school. That night, the principal told the other nuns about the woman who insisted the school accept her son because she needed to work. One of the nuns asked the principal the name of this boy who wanted to start school. The principal said, "Clifford," and the nun asked her if he had a brother named Daniel. "Daniel," the nun said, "is *very* smart. If the brother is anything like him, he'll have no trouble in school." The next day, the principal sent a note home with my brother, telling my mother to bring me down to Mission School. With that, I started a year early and eventually graduated at age sixteen.

I got my first job in 1933, when I was only seven years old. One day Miss Norton, the receptionist and telephone operator at New England Baptist Hospital, met my mother and asked her to send her son up to the hospital. She said that she could give him a job selling magazines outside. In those days, visiting hours were limited to an hour a day — weekday afternoons from three to four and Saturday afternoons from two to three. My brother, who was thirteen, already had a job delivering the *Boston Shopping News*.

My mother asked me if I wanted the job at the hospital. I said, "Sure," and got a note from my father excusing me from school fifteen minutes early so I could go to work. When I first reported to Miss Norton, she asked, "Where's your brother?" I explained that he was already working, so my mother sent me. She was surprised because I was so young, but I got the job anyway.

I sold the magazines for five cents a copy — *Liberty, The Saturday Evening Post*, and *Ladies Home Journal*. That first week, I got twenty-five cents. I brought the money home to my mother. In those days you could buy two quarts of milk for a quarter. I didn't even think of spending it on myself.

I sold those magazines for a few years. Eventually I took over my brother's paper route. Everything I earned, I gave to my mother. If I wanted to go to the movies or a show, I learned to ask my mother.

My father would say, "Take plenty of money," as I was going off somewhere, but he never had any. He was out of work for years, but he did get some short-term jobs through the Works Progress Association, the WPA. Finally he got a job as a clerk at Jordan Marsh department store. By that time, my mother was working as a chambermaid at Simmons College. She had the summers off; that was the best thing.

Meanwhile, I took after my mother and found my own work. My first summer job was at Fenway Park in 1941, when I was in high school. A neighbor's son managed the concessions at Fenway. She sent me over there, and I got the job. I started out with tonic—that was the heaviest—and then moved up to ice cream. In those days they called us "hustlers" because we had to hustle to make any money.

On my first day, I filled out an application, got a white uniform, and went down to the storage room where they gave me a carrier that held about fifteen thick glass bottles of Coke. Once I got my carrier, which had a bottle opener attached, I headed up to the stands. Then I was on my own. For each bottle I sold—at fifteen cents each—I earned one-and-a-half cents.

As time went by, I learned how the other boys were able to make more money. When their trays were half-empty, they went to the men's room and emptied half of the full bottles into the empty ones. Then they filled the bottles with water, so the fans were drinking watered-down Coke, and the hustlers were making a full fifteen cents on some of those bottles. In those days, that was quite a bit of money.

After about a month, I started selling ice cream. Each box cost ten cents; you'd get a penny commission. Some of the boys who worked there would gather the empty boxes the fans had thrown away, clean them up, and get credit for food they didn't sell. They would make forty cents if they turned in four empty boxes, which was a lot of money back then. Bringing back those empty boxes wasn't right. It wasn't exactly stealing but it wasn't honest, and I couldn't do it. I never cheated at school, either. If I didn't know something, I'd say so.

My mother and father taught me right from wrong. Once when I was small, my father came home upset. He had met a neighbor, Mr. McMahon, on the streetcar. When they got off, my father stopped to buy tobacco at Staples, a little variety store in Brigham Circle. Mr. McMahon went in with him. When they got back to McMahon's house, the man pulled two eggs out of his pocket, and said, "Take these, this is your share," and gave them to my father. While my father was buying his tobacco, Mr. McMahon had stolen the eggs. My father, horrified that he was an accomplice to the crime, handed the eggs back to the man and walked away, stunned.

There were hard times but it didn't bother us; we always had enough to eat. We played with other kids in the neighborhood, and we went to church every morning and twice on Sundays. That influenced me, too.

In December 1941, the war started and my brother went into the service. The next year I went to work in the North End, at North Station. The boss wanted to hire someone who was eighteen, so I told him that I had been born in 1924, which made me two years older. My job was to stuff these things called "mounties," the four corners that held pictures in place, into envelopes. We were busy, and sometimes the boss asked me to stay late and work overtime. When my friend Joe asked to stay late, the boss told him, "You can't stay because you're too young." Joe said, "Too young? I'm nine months older than he is!" The boss asked me, "How old are you really?" I told him the truth, but he let me stay until the end of the summer anyway. In 1944, I joined the navy. That's what everybody was doing, so that's what I did.

NO EASY JOB

Rita Rogers

My husband and I had eleven children together, five girls and six boys. He died suddenly in April 1956, one year and ten days after my youngest daughter was born. He was thirty-two years old.

I had met my husband through my cousin. They grew up together in Chelsea, and he came to visit her after he got out of the navy in World War II. His name was Thomas, but we called him Junior even though he was the third Thomas in his family. He was very cute, and at first he tried to take my sister out, but my sister didn't want to go with him. He was five foot five with a medium frame. We dated for almost a year. One day we were walking down the street and this guy who knew him said, "Why don't you just kiss the lady and get it over with?" He was right, too, because Thomas was getting on my last nerve. We got married then, when I was eighteen years old.

My husband worked for the Massachusetts Department of Conservation (MDC). He was the first black person to work for the MDC, first at Columbia Point, and he cleaned up the parks. It was a good job back then, and he liked working outside.

Raising children alone was no easy job. I thank God for all the help I got sometimes. Right after my husband died, the teachers in the Paul A. Dever Elementary School took up a collection to help me along those first few months. The teachers all knew me because I always went to parent-teacher conferences. I was always there, year after year. The money they raised helped me cope while I was getting my husband's pension settled, and I will always be grateful for that help.

I also knew how to stretch a dollar, particularly when I needed clothes for all those kids. I was a regular at the Dollar Days sales at Jordan Marsh. Sometimes people gave me things, but most of the time, I had to shop. I would go there alone and fill up two big bags of clothes. I would fill up one bag and pay for it, then put it in a locker at the train station so I could go back to get some more. I discovered that the boys' dungarees were cheaper than the dungarees in the girl's department. After that, I bought pants only in the boys department. At the end of the day, my kids met me at the train station to help carry all those bags home to where we lived in Columbia Point housing.

I also worked nights. I worked from eight in the evening until five in the morning every day. At eight o'clock each night I laid out all the clothes for my kids to wear the next day at school, and in the morning I got home in time to feed them and walk them across the street to school. We lived in a seven-room apartment. They had big apartments in Columbia Point, so I had five bedrooms for the eleven kids.

I had a good job answering the phone at the Columbia Point Health Center. There was a doctor on call, but he wasn't in the health center. If a patient had to go to the hospital, the driver took them to the hospital, to Tufts or New England Medical Center. I worked on one of those old-fashioned switchboards where you pulled the connection out and plugged it back in. It was old even then. The work was sometimes boring. Some days I worked like heck and others I was bored stiff because the phone didn't ring. We had two floors. The clinic was a converted three-story apartment house. I found three or four desks and put them together. I could sit up there and crochet. One year I made hats for my kids and my grandchildren. A couple of times, we brought in a TV to watch for part of the night.

They had a guard to watch the place because of the medical equipment, and there was money in there, too. One time, I nearly got robbed. That night the driver had come to pick me up a little later than normal, although I lived a few blocks away. When I was coming into the clinic, a man jumped me and tried to grab my pocketbook. I can see that black leather purse right now. The funny thing is that the chain constantly came off that purse, and he was yanking hard on it. He was a young fellow, and I said to him, "You're not getting my pocketbook." I didn't know that he had already robbed the people in the clinic. He'd come in under some pretext that he was sick. Later I found out that he'd had a gun.

With all those kids, I needed to be strict. One night I had a hunch that something was wrong at home, so I called from work at midnight. My daughter answered the phone and told me that the rest of the kids couldn't come to the phone because they were asleep.

I still thought something was wrong, so I asked the driver to take me home right then, and I found that the kids were not at home. My daughter had lied to me, and she was there alone. The rest of them had gone off to what they called "the penthouse." It was the seventh floor of a building down the street where they could get access to the elevator shaft. A child had recently been killed riding the elevators. I told my daughter, "You better get down the street and find your brothers and sisters. If they don't get home quickly, I've got a baseball bat. I got to kill me some kids." I did a nutty on them.

She ran off and told one of the neighbors, "My mother is losing her mind." I said to that neighbor, "There's nothing wrong with me. I haven't lost my senses; I found my senses." I told my kids, "From now on, you earn everything you get. If you don't earn it, you don't get it." Before, when I would tell them to clean up or do the dishes and they wouldn't do it, I'd do it for them. From then on I wanted to know where everybody was all the time. Used to be that as soon as I left, they left. After that, it all changed.

My kids were good most of the time. My older boys worked. Donald delivered papers. Paulie helped out a neighbor doing chores. Three of my children were the first black members in the drum and bugle corps, called the Brigadiers. Two played drums and one carried a flag. I worked for the corps as a volunteer.

I also knew how to feed a lot of kids, and that came in handy when my children brought their friends over, which was nearly every day. Later my grandchildren did the same, bringing their friends home to eat. Sometimes these kids came to visit and I could tell that their parents didn't feed them. I gave them sandwiches and milk, or whatever I had. Peanut butter went a long way. I used to go to Kennedy's to get homemade peanut butter, where you could buy it by the quart, and really good butter. I fed them all. Sometimes I even combed their hair. I was shocked to hear that some kids hadn't eaten because their parents had been out partying and didn't have money left over for food. I didn't feel that was right. My mother and father taught me to be generous. When I was young, kids came to our house all the time to eat, and we had plenty of food because my father always bought fifty-pound bags of potatoes that my mother cooked with onions. My father bought big fish at the wharf, a big haddock or butterfish wrapped in newspaper. Back then we had ice-boxes. I had five brothers and two sisters. My mother was always feeding the kids in the neighborhood, but it was a smaller neighborhood back then, near Dudley Square in Roxbury.

My father never said, "I love you," but he knew what a happy home was. My mother always cooked good food and had a good attitude about life no matter what happened. I tried to give these things—good food and a good attitude about life—to my children, grandchildren, and great-grandchildren.

TOUGH CHOICES

Blanche Sabina

My parents were born in Poland and immigrated to the United States before World War I. They lived in Weymouth before moving to Hyde Park. I was born in Hyde Park and went to the Fairmount Elementary School. I had two brothers and I was the only girl.

My best friends from childhood were Anna Lynch, Rita Scapaci, Pat Duggan, Kay White, and Wanda Wysocki. When it was very hot, we played under the grapevine in the Scapaci's backyard. Mrs. Scapaci always made us oatmeal cookies and brought them out to us under the grapevine. To this day, I have never tasted an oatmeal cookie as delicious as hers. As youngsters, we never got into trouble because we were always playing dodge ball, jacks, pickup sticks, and hopscotch.

We walked together to Hyde Park High. On Sundays, we'd go together to the Howard Johnson's in Blue Hills. If we wanted a hot dog, we walked to Simco's in Mattapan just to save a nickel. Although many of these friendships ended when we got married or

when others moved away, we still remember one another during the holidays.

I graduated from Hyde Park High with the class of 1944. I was accepted to the Forsyth Dental School, but I was only seventeen years old and I had to wait another year before being allowed to work on teeth. My guidance counselor thought I could go to IBM school in Copley Square across from the Boston Public Library. I went with two other girls from Hyde Park. I loved everything about automation in IBM. I worked with all types of IBM equipment and retired after forty-five years.

When I first started to work on IBM machines, they were very large and made loud clanking noises. We had boards with holes and long wires that we had to plug into different sections. Our reports ran off these huge machines. I learned how to work a keypunch machine. We made long bars and notched them to stop at different sections. There were no letters; we only had numeric pads. We had to learn to punch alphabetically. We punched these holes on cards that had eighty columns. This is how automation started.

We progressed to drums and cards, then tapes, and finally computers. Nowadays, laptops and iPhones take the place of a twenty-by-eight-foot room filled with the huge machines. When I worked with these noisy machines, they became very hot. In summer, if the temperature rose above ninety degrees, we had to shut the machines down and call it a day. The air temperature around these huge mainframes had to remain very cold. In the winter, when we worked with computers we wore heavy sweaters and jackets.

I worked at Filene's in retail, purchasing, and payroll. I progressed and worked at Sturtevants' and later with Westinghouse in Hyde Park. That job involved payroll and everything pertaining to the making of fans and equipment used in underground tunnels. I also worked with a service bureau and learned all about stocks, bonds, and retail. I found that I loved variety. When I worked for Lumber Insurance Company, I helped to design a system for automobiles.

IBM approached me because of this system and offered me a position as a trouble-shooter. I was to help companies that were having trouble with their productivity. My territory would spread from Boston to Cape Cod.

I hesitated because I had three small children, but they offered me a nurse to care for my little ones. It was a wonderful opportunity. Then I found out I was pregnant with my fourth child. My husband had lost his job and it was a very hard time in our marriage. I had to make a very big decision; it was a very unsettling time in my life. I had to turn down their offer.

I received two other important opportunities for advancement. One night I was driving through the Fenway on my way to work and I was rear-ended by an elderly gentleman. He pleaded with me not to report the accident, saying that he would pay for the damages. I agreed and forgot about it.

He was a very successful businessman who checked into my background. When he found out how skilled I was, he offered to bring me on to his company. I said I wouldn't leave my first company because they gave me mothers' hours, and school and summer vacations off.

My boss had retired from Lumber and became head of data processing for the town of Needham. He asked me to join him and bring automation to town hall. When he retired, he offered me his job. He was convinced that I could do it, but I knew I couldn't attend all the night meetings and selectman meetings. I still had four children at home so I had to turn it down. I taught ninety people to keypunch and to work with automation.

I declined all three opportunities for career advancement for the same reason: to raise my family and care for my ailing husband. I made the best decision for my family and for myself. I would always be a mom for my children. I never looked back. I ended up being a keypunch operator and a verifier. Nevertheless, I felt fulfilled. All four of my children became successful. My oldest daughter is a private secretary. Another daughter has a master's degree and teaches high school English. One son is a bakery manager and the other is a successful salesman.

As a result of my many years using my hands for automation, I developed repetitive motion syndrome and I wear splints every night. I also don't have a computer because I know if one was available, I would spend hours enjoying it but it would cause more damage to my health and hands.

When I turned forty, I realized I had other desires to fulfill. I wanted to travel with my husband and friends. Between the ages of forty and fifty, I traveled during my vacations to Poland, Greece, England, Ireland, Russia, Israel, and the whole of the United States and Canada.

I have had a very full and rich life with no regrets. My children are always there for me — more than I expected.

HYDE PARK

Rich with Love

SINGING WITH THE SAINTS

Anna Adams

I lived in the Mission Hill Housing Project growing up. I went to Mission School, which was swell. It was nice wearing a uniform because we could all wear the same thing; we didn't have much, but we got along. In the projects, I became friends with a girl named Kay. She lived in the apartment next door, and we became close. Because my grandmother lived in Ireland, Kay's grandmother was like mine, too. She would take us both to the movies and supper, and we thought that was great. When Kay was in the third grade her parents separated, and she went to live on the other side of Roxbury. Still, we kept in touch, and used to call each other on one of the old party lines—you had to wait for your ring.

When I was in the seventh or eighth grade in the late 1940s, I hung out with a group of seven girls in the neighborhood. We all went to school together, and we called ourselves the Saints. The group included my sister Theresa and my friend Kay, who were both a year younger than the rest of us. Eventually Kay moved back to the neighborhood and became my best friend, as she still is today.

There was a songbook that came out once a week called *Hit Parade*, named for the popular radio and TV show, and one of us would get a quarter from her mother to buy a book. The seven of us girls would each have it for a turn overnight to learn the songs. We'd hear the songs on the radio and the neighbors would come out on a summer's evening to listen and tell us we were so wonderful. Singers like Perry Como and Patti Page sang on that radio, and we'd sing along. I loved Perry Como and "Don't Let the Stars Get in Your Eyes" was my favorite song. The neighbor women would come out about eight in the evening and we'd sing something for them, and sometimes they sang with us. They thought that was a pleasant way to spend the evening.

During those long summers we led a wonderful life. Everyone was poor, but the Saints were close. We took the boat to Nantasket Beach; we'd get a ride to Atlantic Pier and the boat cost a quarter. They had an amusement park there called Paragon Park and you could ride all the rides for two dollars and twenty-five cents. There were thousands of people—we would have to stand in line for a half hour to ride—but just being there or knowing we were going there was great.

We'd ask, "Which ride do you want to go on first, the bumper cars?" We loved to bump into other cars, and we went on the roller coaster even though it was scary. We'd say, "I'll never go on that again," but we would because we didn't want to be called chicken. Then we'd split a pizza.

They had a piano on the boat, and someone played so that we could sing along and dance. The boat was packed with people our age—fourteen, fifteen, and sixteen—all dancing and having a good time. We would come home exhausted after running around and riding on all the rides at Paragon Park.

A few years ago I went to Nantasket with a seniors' group. We went to a restaurant and had clams, and they played the old songs, but the amusement park was gone. Today it's just a high-rise. Still, it's joyful. I tried to remember what it was like.

We did lots of other things too. Sometimes we went down to the "Y" on Huntington Avenue to hang out with a group of boys called the Spades. We went bowling there in the evening and they set up the pins for us. The Spades were on the basketball and football teams at school, and we went to the games to cheer them on, but they weren't really our boyfriends. Girls didn't play sports then, and we didn't try to be cheerleaders; we felt we had to be working.

There was a Howard Johnson's nearby, and they were famous for their twenty-eight flavors of ice cream. We worked our way down the list each month and had one sugar cone a day. Then we started to worry about putting on weight, so we just had toast and tea. Around that time several of us got jobs at J.J. Newbery's on Massachusetts Avenue. We worked a full nine-hour day and earned about seven dollars each, then went across the street and spent a whole day's pay on dinner.

After high school, most of us got married. We were bridesmaids in one another's weddings, and some of the girls moved away. One girl moved down to Marshfield, another went down to Quincy. My friend Sis and her husband moved to New Jersey, and then to Chicago. Kay moved to Malden when she got married and we started to get together again. One of the girls passed away. The others are still around the area, but I mostly see my sister Theresa and Kay.

Today Kay and I call each other, just to talk. "What are you doing today?" I'll ask. "Is it raining in Malden?" She comes to visit almost every Sunday. She calls at nine, to tell me she's leaving, and then she comes by, with a half-dozen donuts or muffins. At eleven, we call Theresa, and meet at the restaurant down the street. Sometimes we go to the cemetery to visit our mothers' graves.

In the summer, we walk around, or sit on a bench in the neighborhood, just like in the old days, except now we just talk instead of sing.

THE FIRST DATE

Jo-Anne Palomba

During the summer feasts, the North End is always filled with music, pushcart vendors, parades, and processions. I grew up with those tributes to the Italian patron saints. Our street was narrow, barely a car-width wide, not that anyone had a car, but from our front window, you could see the colored lights of the feast banners, and people coming and going. My friends and I walked around, shopped, and stopped at the quahog wagon to slurp down raw quahogs with a squeeze of lemon. It was a great place to live in the forties and fifties. A group of us who grew up together in the North End still get together on birthdays. One of those friends, Annette, takes credit for matching me up with my husband.

It was July 27, 1952. The North End was celebrating the Feast of St. Joseph. The statue of St. Joseph was being carried through the streets and people pinned money onto the ribbons hanging off of it. Some of the older ladies walked barefoot through the procession in tribute. Children marched in the parade. I remember the smell of sausages, peppers, and onions on twin-bread. All the restaurants

brought their food outside; vendors sold dried nuts hanging on strings (Indian nuts and pistachios), and also *ceci* (dried chickpeas). Soup to nuts, the vendors had it all including pastries. They sold *zeppoli,* a St. Joseph pastry, *cannoli,* and *parigini,* a tiered pastry with yellow cream and sponge cake. I had walked around with Annette, Rocky, and Remo.

Annette and Rocky, her boyfriend at the time, had arranged for Remo to ask me out so that we would go on a double date. Remo was a kid from the neighborhood; we had gone to kindergarten and first grade together, and were classmates all through elementary school and junior high. He lived on Hanover Street; I lived on Hanover Avenue. Of course, I had to ask my parents because I was just fourteen.

We went to the Astor Theatre downtown to see *High Noon,* starring Grace Kelly and Gary Cooper. It was a matinée and we all sat together in the balcony. I wore a white eyelet dress with a little jacket. Remo thought I was the cat's meow, or whatever we said in those days. He might have put his arm around my seat, but that was all. He wouldn't let me go after that.

We didn't kiss. Our date was in July; we did not kiss until November. We walked a girlfriend home one day, lingered in the hallway, and he gave me that first little quick kiss on the lips. He was more excited about it in those days than I was.

After we had graduated from junior high, he went to Dorchester High and I went to Girls High. My family moved to Jamaica Plain, so Remo came to visit every day or every other day, whenever he could. It was a good thing my parents liked Remo because he was always around. He worked at Excellent Sweet Shop after school, and would come see me afterward. Remo traveled back and forth on train, bus, and streetcar to spend time with me. Then he'd go home and call me, and we'd talk on the phone for an hour. His father even put a little padlock on the rotary phone so Remo wouldn't be able to dial. We got around that though — if you jiggled the connection button, the operator would come on and he'd say, "Would you help me get this number: Lafayette 3-4047" and she would connect the call.

His parents were older than my parents; Remo was the baby of the family and I was the oldest of my family. They weren't too excited about him dating anybody; they figured he'd stay home for a while, but he didn't. Remo even came to visit me on my last day at summer camp and brought me a big box of chocolates from work. My father was not too happy. I think he didn't want us to get so serious so soon.

Remo was always there for me — I guess you could say he was smitten. He was always ready to go anywhere, or do anything. He wrote me a letter when we were sixteen. It said, "Dear Jo-Anne, I am writing this letter to tell you that I love you and that you are going to be my wife. Love, Remo." It was just a little note on a plain piece of paper that he handed to me one day. I wish I still had it; I don't know if my mother found the letter and threw it out or what, but I never could find it again.

When we were twenty years old, we had been going together so long that we just decided to get married. We got married April 27, 1958, at the St. Thomas Aquinas Church in Jamaica Plain. My dress had long lace sleeves; the outer skirt was smooth, with ruffles in the front. I think of it as a Cinderella dress. Our reception was held in the Charter Room of the Liberty Mutual Building downtown, with about two hundred friends and family members. We had a live band with a great singer, Jimmy Stella, and our first dance was to "Melody of Love." I don't know how my parents were able to give me such a beautiful wedding. We spent our honeymoon in New York City, where it rained and rained and rained. We went out to different restaurants, and visited the United Nations and the Empire State Building.

As of April 27, 2009, we have been married fifty-one years. Fifty-one Thanksgivings and Christmases together, fifty-one new years, fifty-one birthdays each—boy, are we old! There have been so many happy times, and a few sad and scary times, but we made it through to today, thank God. You live through things; you make it if you try.

SURVIVING IN
CLOSE QUARTERS

Maryalice Bellew

I grew up in my grandmother's house in Hyde Park in the 1930s, during the Great Depression. Five of us shared one bedroom: my mother and father, my younger brother Joseph, and my younger sister Frances and I. It was difficult sharing that room. The quarters were very close; none of us had much privacy. It was called an "in-law apartment" because it was attached to the back of the main house and had just one bedroom, a small kitchen with a black iron stove, a combined living/dining room, and a long storage area that held a little bathroom with a toilet and sink. French doors closed off the storage area because it was freezing cold in the winter. When we wanted to bathe, we used my grandmother's tub.

My two older sisters, Virginia and Patricia, shared a bedroom on my grandmother's side of the house. Grandmother's entire house was full. One of my aunts, her husband, and their two children, as well as another aunt also lived in the home. My father wasn't working and the family needed a place to live. At one time he worked for

the railroad, but he never went back after the workers all went out on strike. I don't know when my family moved into my maternal grandmother's house, but we didn't move out until I was ten.

I don't know how my mother managed. She never talked about the difficult times with us. I guess it was difficult for most people at that time, but I never heard her complain about anything. She seemed to just accept the way things were and adjusted to the problems in her life. She often said, "Waste not, want not, or you may live to say, 'Oh how I wish I had the bread I threw away that day.'" She wasted nothing. She ate the cold, lumpy oatmeal or cream of wheat left over from breakfast for her lunch. For most of my childhood I didn't even know my parents struggled. We always had food and clothing. My mother made a lot of our clothes on an old treadle sewing machine. She would make over old clothes that were too big or too small into something new. I do remember carefully saving any money my grandmother gave me but if my mother needed it, she borrowed it.

Several tall lilac trees stood in grandmother's yard. Frances and I used to sit under them and play school. The backyard also had a bed of poison ivy. One day we had a grand old time marching through it and rubbing it on our skin. I think we wanted to see if we really could get poison ivy. When my father found out he was more than furious at us. He made us wash with Kirkman's brown soap, which everybody used to wash their laundry. Frances got poison ivy, but I never did.

My grandmother had quite a bit of land and my father planted a big vegetable garden. He grew string beans, tomatoes, beets, carrots, and squash. My mother canned and preserved a lot of the vegetables and made her own relish and mincemeat. There was also a grapevine and my mother made her own grape jelly.

Across the street from my grandmother's house was a big field where most of the children in the neighborhood played. I remember Loretta, Josephine, Louise (who we called Cookie), and Marilyn. Frances was always with me, too. We played ball against the old barn next door; we played marbles, climbed trees, and coasted down the hill in the winter. We often played "store." We used small red berries for tomatoes, blades of grass were corn, and rocks were used for money. The commuter rail ran across the back of that field. Every evening, we would wait for the train to pull in and watch all the neighbors coming home from work. We would pick the wild blueberries and blackberries growing along the tracks. As soon as it got dark and the streetlights came on, we knew it was time to go home or my father would be coming to get us soon. When we went home, everybody did.

On Friday nights while my mother was out at the church or at a meeting of the Catholic Daughters or the Ladies Sodality, my father got out his movie projector. He would make popcorn, tack an old sheet up on the wall, and put in a film reel. We all sat and watched cartoons, just like in the movie theater.

On Sunday afternoons, my father took Frances, Joseph, and me for walks around the neighborhood. He would point out buildings that had changed over the years or tell us about the streetcar that ran down River Street when he was a child.

When I was ten, we moved out of my grandmother's house. My father had taken a job as a mechanic at Westinghouse. My parents rented one side of a three-story duplex around the corner for eighteen dollars a month. We had so much more room there. My parents had their own bedroom, my two older sisters shared a room, Frances and I shared a room, and Joseph had his own room in the attic. We could still cut through the backyard to my grandmother's backyard, and play in the field with the other kids. We stayed in this house for the rest of my childhood. When I was in high school, my grandmother's house was sold and she moved in with us. She had been feeble for quite some time, and she died not long after moving in.

In 1953, our landlord sold the duplex. My mother always wanted to own her own house, but she did not want to leave the parish. She and my father bought a house about four doors up the street. Now we had two bathrooms and continuous hot water, which was a treat. By then I was out of high school and working. I brought home twenty-five dollars a week. Twenty dollars went to my parents, and I was allowed to keep the rest. My mother finally had her own home, but unfortunately she would not enjoy it for very long. She died two years later at fifty-four years of age. That year, 1955, ground was broken to build the new church, and the church minstrel show was dedicated to her.

Many things have changed in the neighborhood. The commuter rail stop has long since been removed, and the big field now holds a public storage facility, but I still live in my parents' house today with my two children. I have lived in four different houses in the same neighborhood where I was born in 1933.

THE WICKER ROCKING CHAIR

Maryalice Bellew

My grandmother had a black wicker rocking chair with flowered cushions. It sat in her kitchen beside the window, and she rocked in it all the time. She could see the house next door and she would watch us with our friends playing ball in their yard. I remember my mother nursing my baby brother to sleep in that chair. When she rocked, it would put her and the baby in her arms to sleep. When grandmother's house was sold, the rocking chair moved to our kitchen. My bedridden grandmother lived with us for a while. On some days my mother could convince her to join us in the kitchen, and mother and I would walk with her slowly, step by step down the stairs, so she could sit in that rocking chair. Years later, after I was married, this chair ended up in my bedroom near the window. It is part of the family. The rocker on it is now gone. You might say that after so many years of rocking, the old chair just got tired.

MAINE COURSE

Alta Kilton McDonald

"Just a little to port. Okay, now a little to starboard. Pick a point and aim for it. Steady as she goes. Pay attention to the buoys." Daddy is instructing me on how to steer the *Woiee,* a seventy-two-foot sardine carrier built in 1918. It is 1942 and I am eight years old. In the summer when there is a short run to a weir in Machias Bay, I get up before dawn to go downriver with Daddy. Because I'm not tall enough to see over the wheel, he puts me on a wooden box.

I didn't have many toys as a child. I was ashamed of my second-hand bike with its crudely painted black body and its ugly metallic paint on the wheel rims and spokes. I had my heart set on a gleaming red Schwinn. Being aboard the *Woiee* was a good substitute even though it reeked of dead fish, diesel fuel, and dried salty brine. A weir at daybreak was my very own nature movie. Legions of seagulls patrolled overhead crying mournfully. Thousands of sardines shimmered in the blue-black Atlantic, thrashing frantically about. Maybe they realized that they had been duped into swimming into a weir at high tide, being captured there hours later when the tide went down. It was always an even bigger thrill to spy large eels or mackerel among the sardines.

I loved the fo'c'sle (or forecastle), living quarters for Daddy and Captain Ernest Libby. I thought of it as a nautical playhouse with its mini wood-burning stove, small pots, foldout table, four bunks, and many tidy compartments for storage. Daddy produced memorable meals from a can of corned beef shredded and fried with a little onion, thickened with flour and water. He served it with ragged drop biscuits the size of an egg made from flour, baking powder, water, and shortening. According to my father, the builder came up with the name *Woiee* by using the first letter of each of his children's names. I used to imagine the names of these five children. Were they boys — William, Otis, Ira, Edward, Eric? Were they girls — Wendy, Olive, Irene, Eleanor, Elaine? Or was it some combination of boys and girls? Or was this one of Daddy's tall tales?

In 1937, my parents, Charles and Adelaide Kilton, bought their first and only home for one thousand dollars on the crest of Trafton's Hill in Machiasport, Maine. Built in the late 1800s, it was the ultimate fixer-upper: no indoor plumbing, no central heat, and cracked plaster walls. It sat on top of a steep bank. The lot wasn't desirable. Giant rocks had been deposited by a glacier thousands of years before. There was also a large outcropping that I called my "mountain." The most outstanding feature of our home was a view of Machias Bay and Round Island. I often perched on the bank to watch a parade of working boats: sardine carriers, skiffs for clam diggers, and two four-masted schooners, the *Lucy Evelyn* and the *Lillian Kerr.*

Mama and Daddy were self-reliant and work-oriented. They were very modern for their time. They shared in my care and fixing up the house. On one occasion they decided to cover a cracked plaster ceiling with panels of Cellotex, a heavy fiber material. In order to fasten the panels, strips of wood had to first be fastened to the plaster. Daddy would hammer while Mama held the wood strips. At one point their signals were confused and I watched with horror as the strip struck my mother on the head, stunning her and knocking off her glasses.

In 1937, my mother also resumed her career as a teacher at a local one-room school. She despaired over the lack of intellect in her students whose parents were hamstrung by poverty, seasonal work, and bleak futures. One night in an effort to lend some humor to the situation, Daddy said, "Just remember, Adelaide, that two half-wits don't add up to a whole wit."

I knew that I wasn't a pretty child because of my straight hair and many freckles. Grammy Kilton reinforced this by comparing me unfavorably with my female cousins who had fair skin and naturally curly hair. I tended to be a little too plump and was teased about that. I didn't ever think that I was homely, but rather settled into thinking that I was a little plain. I hated my hair. Mama would take me to a barbershop and say, "Shingle it up the back and cut it with just the tip of the ear showing." On special occasions she would coax a little curl using a curling iron. She would then make a tight pigtail and add a three-inch-wide taffeta bow.

I didn't try to conform to the work ethic of the old house. I loved to play by the hour on my "mountain" with my imaginary family, the Lukens. They were named for vegetables: Tomato, Lettuce, Carrot, and Peas. One day I told Mama that I heard Tomato on the radio. During spring grass-burning in the upper field the night before, all of us kids smoked a dried hollow reed. Could I have been under the influence of some kind of hallucinogenic substance?

Daddy would become upset with me for reading too much. "People who read too much is about as worthwhile as tits on a boar hog," he'd say. I read a number of series books: Pollyanna, Cherry Ames, and Grace Harlow from Mama's childhood collection and Horatio Alger from Daddy's. Our only access to library books was from a large wooden box that was delivered to elementary schools from the Maine State Library in Augusta. Mother tried valiantly to teach me to help with canning at the end of summer. One time she said, "Now it is time to put your rubbers on." I went to the back hall and came back wearing my galoshes. She didn't find humor in that, but she hadn't said anything about jar rubbers. At one point during World War II, I was convinced that, under the cover of night, Nazis had landed on the shore of Machias Bay and had substituted Gestapos for my loving parents.

Despite the regimentation at home, I had the run of the village in the summer. At high tide, Cora, Becky, Dicky, Emery, and I could swim in Machias Bay. To get to the beach we just crossed the road to trudge down a steep descent through the cemetery. Along the way we passed through centuries of Maine history: the burial plots of my ancestors who were sea captains engaged in the coastwise trade from Maine to the Caribbean; a monument to Captain Peterson's wife who died in the West Indies; and a midden of clam shells left by Native Americans long before the early settlers arrived in northeast Maine. We were told that when poor Mrs. Peterson became deathly ill at sea, she begged Captain Peterson to bury her in Machiasport. To honor her wishes, he transported her home in a keg of rum.

During the wintertime when Mama taught school, my father would take me to hang out around the wood stove with his friends at the general store. I would listen to crude language, but could not differentiate between accepted and forbidden words. I will never forget the time when Aunt Toncie came for an elegant lunch of lobster salad. The table was set with fine linen and highly polished silver. I was freshly scrubbed, hair curled, bow perched on my head, and wearing a red and white smocked dress from the Sears Roebuck catalog. I looked at Aunt Toncie and said in my most polite tone, "Please pass the butter, you damn bitch." In an instant I was whisked from the table and my mouth washed out with a bar of Fels Naptha, a harsh laundry soap.

Life in a small coastal Maine town was all about surviving. We never thought of ourselves as poor. During the summer we raised vegetables and lived grandly on fresh fish. "Short" lobsters below the legal limit were in plentiful supply. Mama would boil them in a large canner and neatly stack dozens of them in tidy rows in our Frigidaire refrigerator. For a special treat she would spend hours picking out the tiny morsels she called sweetmeats and make a most elegant lobster stew. I was instructed to refer to lobster as "fish" in case an inspector appeared. Mackerel often arrived with the sardine catch.

As kids we went to the factory with a bucket to pick them from the conveyor belt that took the sardines upstairs for packing. Mama canned them with delicious pickle brine.

During World War II we raised a personable pig named Hortense. Cousin Jimmy and I loved observing her by the hour in her pen and watching her gobble up loads of table scraps. Daddy regularly measured her girth and compared her with neighbors' pigs. When Hortense was almost ready for slaughter, she rooted under her pen and escaped. Daddy and his friends had a dickens of a time trying to capture her as she was both wily and slippery. It was very emotional that winter when we ate Hortense. As hard as we tried, none of us could hide tears as we ate roast pork, pork chops, and bacon.

Now, in the early part of the twenty-first century, Machiasport has changed dramatically. The sardine canneries are gone, and the waterfront is no longer active except for a few intrepid clam diggers with their skiffs. Affluent baby boomers, in search of undeveloped waterfront property, have arrived. Machiasport even has a gated community at Yoho Head, choice waterfront acreage. The two venues of my childhood have been glamorized. The old homestead has been thoroughly renovated and reoriented on the lot so that a daylight basement could be built. There is an ample back deck over the pen where Hortense was raised and jammed close to the "mountain" where my imaginary family, the Lukens lived. The *Woiee* still exists. She has been converted to a small luxury yacht that sailed out of Newport, Rhode Island. She is currently for sale for $170,000 on the Web.

THE BIG FOUR
AND ESMERALDA:
A SISTERHOOD

Kathleen Dash

H ello, little girl, will you be my friend?" Those were the first words Amelia ever spoke to me, and we formed a friendship that day that has lasted nearly seventy years. Amelia McAllister Reddick was three years old and I was four. My family was moving into an apartment on Symphony Road in the Back Bay neighborhood. Our neighborhood was inhabited by Irish, Greek, Italian, West Indian, southern black, and Jewish people, and seemingly every other ethnicity. Amelia lived just down the street and became the sister I never had. We dressed alike and told everyone that we were twins. It did not matter that she was tall and thin and I was short and chubby.

My mother was very strict. She did not allow me to play outside very often, but we could roller-skate on the sidewalk in front of our apartments. As we got older Amelia and I visited the rose garden

55

in the Fens for picnics in the summer. We entered the world of Girl Scouts (Amelia) and Camp Fire Girls (me). Amelia took classes at the Museum of Fine Arts, while I discovered ballet and spent many happy hours at the dance studio of Harriet Hoctor, a famous dancer. On Sunday afternoons, we went to the movies at the Uptown Theatre on Huntington Avenue and joined the other teenagers that gathered in the balcony.

One day a boy that I had met at the theatre came to visit me when no one else was home. He was just a friend, but I was showing him the upright piano in my room when I heard my mother come in the front door. I tried to push to him out the door without her seeing, but she saw us and there was hell to pay. Upon learning of my trouble, the boy came over to the house on his own and apologized to my parents. That was chivalry. After that incident, my mother and father believed there were too many boys in the neighborhood, and that I was too interested in them for my own good so we had to move to Roxbury.

What made moving to Roxbury tolerable was meeting the teenagers at the Dudley Street elevated station. I no longer walked to school, but took a bus and a train. Everyone gathered at the station to greet one another. This is how I met Joan Patrice. She didn't attend the same school as I did, but we became acquaintances. After graduating from Girls' Latin I went on to Boston Clerical School, where Carol Contee and I became fast friends. Joan and Carol knew one another, and Amelia had attended Sunday school with Carol, but "the Big Four" did not become closely knit until marriage and children brought us together.

By the early 1960s, we all lived in Roxbury, were married, and had nine children among us. Joan, Carol, Amelia, and I spent blissful afternoons in Franklin Park jumping rope and acting worse than the kids. I tied a rope around my son and attached the other end to a tree so he wouldn't wander off. I think that would be considered cruelty to children in this day and age. We spent a good amount of time visiting back and forth between our houses, but most of the time we

The Big Four: Amelia (top left), Joan (top right), Kathy (bottom left), and Carol (bottom right)

went to Joan's home where we watched the soaps, played cards, and ate raisin rummy cookies — the closest we came to hard liquor. If we spent too much time in Franklin Park and were late for the soaps, we ran to my house because I lived right across the street.

Summer weekends found us all, including husbands, at Scusset Beach in Bourne, Massachusetts. Our four families, including the nine children, would descend on the lovely, pristine beach with baby furniture, ice chests, beach chairs, umbrellas, and anything else we thought we needed. We trekked across half the beach to get to the perfect spot. One day, my husband and one of his friends decided to go fishing. After a few hours, we saw the two of them walking back. Where was the car, a new Oldsmobile? And where were the fish? The car was cracked up on the side of the road. This, of course, led to a heated family discussion. Thank goodness for my husband's sister and brother who lived in Mashpee and let us spend the night. Eventually, the whole incident blew over and we resumed more pleasant times at Scusset Beach.

At some point, the Big Four realized we needed our own car for getting around town. My husband, Randall, came through and found us a Ford Fairlane 500. Although "Esmeralda" was my car, Carol drove her and we were all happy as pigs in mud. Carol loved to drive and knew all the routes we needed, so she chauffeured us everywhere. Don't ask me how, but nine kids and four adults fit in that Ford Fairlane. We looked like circus clowns piling out of a little car. Years later, when Esmeralda had worn out from our adventures, I called the towing company and stood in the window as she was towed away. Tears streamed down my cheeks as I mourned the loss of a dear friend.

Amelia, Joan, Carol — each of these women was an integral part of the Big Four sisterhood. Carol was a true confidant that we could go to with any personal problem. She not only tried to give good advice, but she also wouldn't share your problems with anyone else. Joan, on the other hand, could not keep a secret if her life depended upon it. Joan and Carol were the leaders of the group, each one vying for control of whatever activity we had planned. They were the argumentative ones. Amelia always agreed with the winner, no matter what. I was the most laid-back member of the group. My favorite expression to this day is "whatever." The kids, of course, loved Amelia and me because we were more lenient.

Longfellow wrote, "Into each life a little rain must fall," and tragedy struck each of the Big Four over the years. First, Joan's beautiful three-year-old daughter died in an unfortunate accident. Then, Amelia had an illness that almost killed her, and my husband lost both of his legs in an industrial accident. Lastly, Carol died suddenly of cancer. We rallied with each horrific event, but some of life's wounds never heal.

I'm not particularly religious, but I know the Big Four will all be together again. As I age, I look back at my life and thank the Supreme Being for the friends I have had. Although Joan is in a wheelchair, she is still a feisty smart aleck with a heart of gold. Amelia is still the sweet-natured, good friend that she has always been. And although she is gone, we all still talk to Carol and seek her advice.

Rolling with the Punches

THE EARLY DAYS
OF MOTHERHOOD

Barbara Hopwood

I was born in East Bridgewater, Massachusetts, on December 2, 1932. I was told that my mother died giving birth to me but the doctor brought her back to life. Mother had seventeen child-births but only twelve survived. I was the tenth child. After me she had twins, one of whom died. Then she had one more girl.

My oldest sister Dot took care of me because mother was weakened from so many labors. Dot looked after me until she married. She took me everywhere and bought me pretty clothes. She took me on dates and let me stay up late. When she got married, I was about four and I wanted to go and live with her, but she left me to fend for my-self. My older sisters teased me because they knew Dot spoiled me.

After Dot left the house, everything changed. My sisters made me go to bed early and they hid my nice clothes. I had no place to sleep. There were two bedrooms, one had twin beds and the other had a regular bed for five girls. I had to sleep between my two older sisters at the foot of the regular bed.

My father had his own electrical business and worked from sunup until sundown. I can remember the aroma of coffee that he made early in the morning with his oatmeal. On Sundays after church, he would take mother and the girls on his route to pick up his money for the jobs he did. Mother made out the bills and kept track of the jobs. We were the first family in the neighborhood to buy a TV. *The Jack Benny Show* was Dad and Mom's favorite program, and on Sunday nights we would all sit around the living room to watch it.

Mother kept us girls under her wing. First she had two boys, then Dot, followed by four boys, and then five girls. We were not allowed to have friends over. We played with our dolls, creating houses from boxes, cutting holes for windows and making curtains. We also played with cars and made hills with books under the carpet. When Mother and Dot came home from shopping, we stopped playing and put everything away.

It seemed that Mother was always in the basement, washing clothes and hanging them on the clothesline. My sisters and I took turns holding the wet clothes to go through the wringer. Once, my sister Gloria got her hand caught in the wringer. She was screaming but we didn't know how to stop it. Finally Mother came in and stopped the wringer. That was the last time we helped. To cut down on the laundry in summer, she made us wear our bathing suits. We didn't mind because we liked squirting each other with the hose.

There were always mountains of clothes in the sunroom. One hot day, the clothes caught on fire and we had to hose it down to put out the fire. Another time, the kitchen caught on fire. Mother tried to put it out with a scatter rug. She closed all the doors and told us to stay out of the kitchen. I remember my two brothers came to help put out the fire. They took out the stove; the fire department was never called. We had to eat downstairs in the musty basement until the kitchen was fixed. That's when the breakfast nook was added on. The only time I remember Mom and Dad sitting down to eat with us was Thanksgiving and Christmas.

Mother decided it would be a good idea to send me to Miss Hicks' School with my older sister to learn poise and manners. Dot and Mother wanted to get rid of me since I was always getting into mischief and fighting with my sisters. Even though they were the ones who started the fights, I was the one Mother scolded. What Mother said was law. She always knew when we fibbed. We were told not to repeat anything that was said in the house to outsiders because they could not be trusted.

We had a big yard and we all pitched in making vegetable gardens. At harvest time my brother would drive around the garden and we would put the ripe vegetables in the open truck as it moved slowly by us. Sometimes we would jump on the back to have a ride around the garden and back to the house to put away the vegetables. Blueberry bushes, apple trees, and pear trees were everywhere. At Easter my father bought baby chickens and put them in an incubator in the garage. We fed them until they were fat and old enough to kill. My brother had a pig that he had slaughtered when it was fat.

When the war broke out, two of my brothers enlisted in the army, the other two enlisted in the navy, and my sister's husband was a merchant marine. My father became a dollar-a-year man for the navy in Rhode Island. We kept the family house and rented in a project in Quonset Point. Times were tough; food and gas were rationed. Mother put us girls into a convent for a year during the war because we were struggling so much financially. Dot would drive mother over on weekends for visits. I remember they would announce the names to go to the visitor's center and my name was not called. I would cry seeing my sisters go and not me.

When I graduated from Brockton High, I wanted to go to secretarial school in Boston. I knew about the train schedule and Mother said that if I could find my own way to the school and home, I could go. I had visions of getting a good job and marrying the boss. I got all the information Mother requested but we ended in an argument. Mother locked me in the basement until I came to my senses.

While I was in the basement, my older sister who had just graduated from nursing school came down to convince me to take up nursing. She said I could be with her, get away from Mother's clutches. I agreed. The basement did not hold any future for me. I studied very hard to get passing grades.

I met my first husband when I was in nursing school at Long Island Hospital. He was an orderly in the ward where I was assigned. The hospital held dances for the students and staff, and I went with a group of students. I was a saucy gal. I wore tight-fitting clothes and my hair was curly and long. I wore it like Veronica Lake, the movie star, with my hair draped to one side over my eye. I caught Bill's eye at the dance. When I saw him, I knew he was the one for me. I always wanted to have blond, blue-eyed babies. Then we made a date to go for a drive in my car. A couple of weeks later he asked me to marry him. I went home and told my mother and dad. Mother said,

"No, you are not going to marry him. You finish your nursing first or I will call the police and put you away as an unruly child."

I went back to Bill and told him we would have to wait until the next weekend. We got married on November 2, 1952, in New Hampshire by a justice of the peace. Our marriage was a secret and we had no place to live, so we had to go back to our normal routine at the hospital. Meanwhile, Mother and Dad had arranged with the parents of a neighbor for me to marry their son, whom I had dated. I said, "No! I will pick my own man!"

When Bill joined the marines two weeks after we got married, I followed him to Georgia and then to California. Mother called and asked me to come home and finish nursing school. The school did not allow married students so I told her no. When she called to say that my father was dying, I didn't believe her until my brother called and told me my dad was on his deathbed and to get myself home right away. I got home in time to see my dad take his last breath on July 4, 1953.

I stayed at home and worked two jobs to save money for the time Bill would come home. I had an apartment with my two older sisters on the second floor of my brother's carpet business in Brockton. When Bill came home, we got our own apartment.

At first I couldn't have children. My mother had forbidden us to be examined by a doctor until we were married. I underwent surgery to correct my womb and I had a D&C. In March 1957 I had my first blond, blue-eyed boy who weighed nine pounds. I had a total of six children in six years—three of them were blonds.

I put Bill through school to become a detective and he worked all hours but most of the time he was drinking. I raised the children alone and worried about him. He always came home after midnight drunk. I discovered that he was gambling. We never had enough money; I was always asking the mortgage company to extend the payment so we wouldn't lose the house. I was ready to divorce him. I got a separation twice after my youngest daughter was born.

One day in 1972, I was at work and got a call that Mother was really sick. I spent as much time as I could with her since my children were old enough to stay alone. I took care of Mother, getting her medicine, but her heart was weak. On her last night, she asked me to open the blinds so the sun would come in. I told her that it was raining and was going to rain for the rest of the week. She also said that she wanted to be taken out at night, so the neighbors wouldn't know. Everything went according to her plan. I called the doctor and told him she had passed away. He said, "How do you know?" I said, "Her feet are blue and she is not breathing."

In the meantime, Bill was out of work for several years and was unable to support us. After giving him many chances, I decided to divorce him.

I spent my life raising the six children until they married. My baby married in October 1989 and I married George, a man much older than me who treated me well. We moved to Hyde Park when we got married. We had a good fifteen years together until his death in 2004.

BIG CHANGES

Margaret Dunn

The first house I remember was a large ten-room stucco house on thirty acres of land in Wilmington, Massachusetts, where I lived until I was six years old. I had two older brothers and two loving parents. I was my father's "little girlie" and I loved to greet him when he came home from work. He was an Englishman, six feet tall, born in Torpoint, England. He came to America with his family; they owned a stucco business in England. His office was in Boston on Beacon Street and he commuted by train every day.

When I was smaller, I would sit on his lap. He was always dressed in a dark suit and vest. I used to play with the large watch and fob that draped across his chest. My mother came from a large family, born in Scotland, and she had a real Scottish nature, so loving and caring.

My brothers and I had plenty of room to play and we were always outside. I particularly loved to go up the hill in back of our barn and swing with my brothers. Behind the pine knoll was a trail that led to a brook running down the hill. Jack-in-the-pulpits, lady slippers, and skunk cabbage (which I recall had a bad odor) bordered the trail, among other pretty flowers and plants. That was a very memorable place for me and I always wanted to go there with my brothers when we played. It later became part of Route 128. We had a well in the side yard in front of the red barn. We had several barnyard hens, Bantam roosters, and baby chicks. I can recall my father candling the eggs. The egg was put on a hole on top of a box that contained a light bulb and if any flaw appeared, the egg would be discarded. I loved hearing the roosters crow every morning and I can still hear them. We were the only house on the road, except for two dairy farms about a mile away.

We also had a large collie dog that had thirteen puppies the last autumn we were there. My father would let her out of the barn every morning, and the mother and the puppies would race around the pump several times, enjoying their first freedom. Later I recall we had to try and get rid of the puppies, and had them in a large pen on our front lawn. That made me very sad.

That winter, my father passed away. He came home one night after getting his feet wet while coming home from the train. He went to bed with a chill and three days later he died of double pneumonia. There were no antibiotics back then. Around the time my father had passed away, I was in school and apparently not getting my proper sleep, as I must have fallen asleep at my little desk. My thoughtful teacher let me lie down behind her desk in back of the curtain and rest. It was January 1923 and I was six years old.

As difficult as this time was for me, it was much harder for my mother. She was a tiny woman, only five feet tall, and had just had an operation to remove a tumor. After my father's death, she was left

with a very big decision. She had no husband and no income, three children, and poor health. She cried a lot of the time, and could not really get out of bed or take care of us. She did the only thing she could do. She sold our house and sent her children to live with relatives while she recovered. Everything went topsy-turvy for me for a while.

During this time I went to stay with my aunt in Connecticut and went to school there, which terrified me. I was there for about a year, until I moved to Springfield, Massachusetts, to live with another aunt for another year. Meanwhile, my mother was progressing health-wise and our family was reunited at last.

My mother moved to Hyde Park to stay with my aunt and recuperate. When she was better, we got an apartment in Hyde Park where she and my oldest brother went into the real estate business together.

I went to St. Raphael's School in Hyde Park, and many evenings went across the street with my brother to take care of a schoolteacher's furnace. This was in the mid-1920s. He had to shake down the briquettes to get the fire started again because the coals had burned out. He would put new briquettes on top so that the fire would last for another day. It would take quite a while to do that, and we enjoyed many jokes together during our time together. He also worked for the Ecco grocery store on River Street and had a big pushcart to deliver the shopping circulars to houses in the area. My oldest brother was eight years older than I, and he became the man of the house and took on a lot of odd jobs to help the family.

I loved dancing and took many classes. My mother made all of my beautiful costumes for the recitals.

When I was in junior high, my mother bought a three-family house and rented the second and third floors for income. A policeman and his wife rented our second floor, and they owned a radio. I looked forward to going up to their apartment and sitting in front of the radio, enthralled by all the programs. I thought they must be rich, because they owned a radio. (We bought our first one from Burnes Brothers in Cleary Square, I think, "on time" for a dollar per week.)

In 1929 the stock market crashed. The real estate market plummeted. There were no rentals or sales, and times were very bad. In those days we cashed in an empty bottle to get five cents, which was urgently needed, sometimes to buy a loaf of bread. The trolleys ran along Hyde Park Avenue from Forest Hills to Cleary Square and cost five or ten cents. We had little money to spend for clothes and depended on hand-me-downs. The very first coat that I loved was a beige leather jacket that I received for Christmas.

My mother filled in as a teacher for paper-flower–making classes, which were held in the Hyde Park High School Building. One evening she went to a class in Watertown and contracted diphtheria there. She went to the hospital for a month's stay as it was contagious. It was a very long month and my first at "keeping house." I was fourteen years old.

Once in a while my mother worked at Raymond's "where you bought the hat" as a salesperson. I got a kick out of that, going in to see her when she was working there. That was in Boston, and I had to take the elevated train to get there.

She ended up working for a baby doctor in Arlington. She went to people's homes and when the baby and the mother came home from the hospital, she took complete care of them for a month or so. She worked for the doctor and helped care for the babies of people who could afford this luxury.

For years I had watched how my mother managed to support our family. I knew that I wanted to work, too, but in an office as a secretary. I was good at taking shorthand and was known in high school as someone who took dictation from my shorthand teacher who also was on the Board of Trade in Hyde Park. After two years of business school, my first job was working for the State Planning Board and then for the Gillette Company. I was there for thirty-eight years and met many famous sports figures, among them Joe Louis, while working in advertising for the vice president.

When you ask me who I admire most, it's my mother. I wish I could be more like her. She was such a remarkable woman who was faced with a terrific problem and conquered it and moved on to become a successful businesswoman. She was my role model — a great lady who taught me so many wonderful things. Reflecting back on my childhood years, I believe that all of my experiences have helped me in my later years to take a positive attitude and do my best in each situation. After all, isn't that all God would ask?

ROLLING WITH THE PUNCHES

Remo Palomba

I am a survivor. I was born in the North End and my life as a child was good and not so good. I never studied Italian; I picked it up at home listening to my mother and father, as that was all that was spoken in the house. My father was two people—Dr. Jekyll and Mr. Hyde. In Italy, he was a decorated officer in Mussolini's army; he was a war hero. He always smoked stogies and loved to play cards in Paul Revere Park.

My father was very strict. My mother never had a chance to get a word in. My sisters could not come to the dinner table with any kind of makeup. You couldn't speak unless you were spoken to. In other words, you were lucky you could breathe. I had a very rough childhood being punished by my father almost everyday for what reasons, I don't know. Maybe, in his eyes, I wasn't doing the right things, but to me they were. I was abused and so were my sisters and my brother. I was the youngest of nine. We learned how to roll with the punches. I guess we all knew how to survive. We all knew we were going to get beaten with the shaving strap, be kicked at, be punished. There were other things that happened that we weren't prepared for, but I guess the Almighty was watching over us.

But to me, the North End was the greatest place to live. I'm glad God gave me a chance to live there from the forties to the sixties. When I was growing up, kids thought that the North End was always better than the West End and every so often, on a late Saturday night, we used to have a fruit fight. Nothing serious, just one day someone had the idea that we, the North Enders, would go down to the big fruit market at Faneuil Hall at closing time and load up the leftover fruit, some rotten vegetables, and head over to the North End/West End line, near the old Boston Garden. The street is still there and that's where we used to start our so-called Rotten Fight. There were usually about twenty-five to thirty boys on each side, armed with fruit and protecting ourselves with the peach basket covers we used as shields. At first, the police did not allow it but after talking it over, there were a few deals made. It really wasn't a serious fight, just a way to express ourselves and to see who was better. At times someone on either side would get a bloody nose or other bruises from the apples, oranges, bananas, cukes, whatever there was being thrown. It would last an hour or so and sometimes when it was all over we shook hands and called it quits, just like two fighters in the ring. We looked like Spartans with our shields. It was just a way of having fun, that's how we saw it. Then we would clean up the mess, our battlefield, which was one of the deals made. This was one of the high points in my younger days.

One of my favorite foods was polenta. It's made with cornmeal. I used to help my father make it. He made the gravy with meat and red beans. A wooden bread and pasta board that was about three

feet by four feet long was placed in the center of the kitchen table after the polenta was done. We spread it on the board with the sauce on it. In the middle of the board, my father would put a glass with a dollar in it and, at that time, it was like a thousand dollars. The first one to reach it, by eating polenta to the glass in the center, would win it. It wasn't as easy as it sounds. The meal was very filling. The trick was not to drink anything while eating; if you did, you couldn't eat another forkful. One of my older brothers would always win. I never won, as I was very small.

After my father died, my mother was very good to us. She was about five foot three and wore the same clothing that almost every Italian wore then, nothing fancy unless it was an important event. My mother was always in the kitchen cooking; she was a wonderful cook. She also knit, mostly hats, blankets, anything that would come into her mind.

In the forties and fifties, you had to know and think how to survive, not only with your friends but with grownups, the Mafia, the police, the teachers, priests, and nuns. I thank God he made me survive through those times. You learned right from wrong real quick. Make no mistake: it was scary at times. I think about it always, even now that I am seventy-two years young. It was the golden age of my life.

I met my wife in nursery school and have known her ever since. She was my first date, my first kiss, and my first and only love. I got married in 1958 and moved to Jamaica Plain where she and her family had moved. I have lived here ever since.

My advice to anyone who is working is to be yourself and not someone you're not; work like a human being not like a bull; think before you do something. Remember it's your life and be careful and be alert in whatever you do. We're just a number; if anything happens to you, they pick up the phone and call for a new person. Roll with the punches.

GOOD FAMILY, GOOD FRIENDS

John Vaccaro

When my mother was young, she didn't go to school. She stayed at home and helped around the house. When my father left the United States to go to Italy and marry my mother, he was unlucky because the war broke out and he got stuck there, serving in the Italian army for seven years. He got out, and married my mother and brought her to this country where I was born in Dedham, Massachusetts.

My mother had six children in a row, eighteen months apart, every one of us. She had three boys and three girls. I remember my mother always working, washing clothes and cooking. My mother made homemade bread. You could smell it from the street. Every time the teachers came by our house, they would smell the bread and my mother was right there to hand them a loaf. She went through a lot of flour, and in those days, flour sacks were so soft. They were made of cotton that was better than any cloth you could buy, so my mother would make pillowcases out of them, and dresses, too.

The baker, named Ravezini, had a horse and buggy and he would deliver the bread loaves to everyone, and to the Italians, he would deliver flour so that the Italian mothers could make their own bread.

Our regular meals during the week were like a holiday meal today. We had a black oil stove and food was always on it. When any of the neighbors got sick, we would bring a live chicken with the neck sticking out of the bag and the whole family together would go on a visit. When any member of our household got sick, a neighborhood family would come to our house with a chicken ready to cook. Every time we killed a chicken my mother would keep the feathers and use them to stuff the pillowcases she'd made.

My father worked on the railroad, as did my grandfather. When he came home we all had to be at the table to eat supper. God forbid if one of us was not there. My father sat with the boys and my mother sat with the girls. We lived in a two-family house, with my grandmother on one side and my family on the other. There were fences around all the properties. The neighborhood was all Italians. The Germans were in another section. The Irish were in the square and Polish in another area. We were all separate in a way, but were all in the same class. None of us had cars, so we all walked everywhere and everyone knew everyone's name.

I had a lot of fun in school, although I wasn't an A student—more like a C student or sometimes a D student. One of my memories from first grade was the day soldiers came to school to talk to us. We had a soldier visit from World War I and a soldier from the Civil War. A lot of people don't believe me when I tell them this, but remember that this was 1932 and a lot of those soldiers went to war when they were twelve or thirteen years old. They were still alive when I was a kid.

I loved school because I had so many friends and we were always joking around and having fun. Sometimes we had too much fun. One day I got expelled from school. I couldn't come back until I brought one of my parents to the school. I chose my mother, of course, because she couldn't speak or understand English. But she knew enough, as I found out. My teacher told her about me and I denied it all. My mother slapped me across the face and in broken English told me to "shutta uppa you mouth." I was so embarrassed.

When I was in my last year in junior high at the Avery School, my friends went around to make sure I was elected president of our class. The school principal Mr. Brown didn't think I should have been elected president. He wanted someone smarter. The main job of the class president was to present a gift to the school at an all-school assembly. The gift for that year was a radio. The principal asked another student, the smartest one in class, to present the radio at the assembly and my name was never mentioned. However, when the class photos were taken, I was seated in the middle of the class, just as the president would be.

In high school, my best friend was Frankie Madonna. We did everything together. One evening, he and I were working at two different shoe stores when some of our friends called us to go swimming at nine o'clock when we closed. Not knowing that the water was over our heads, Frankie and I jumped in. Neither of us could swim. The rest of the gang had jumped in and was already swimming to the other side of the river. Frankie and I struggled to stay above water.

No one heard us yelling. I did the dog paddle and tried to save my friend, but I couldn't. He held onto me, and I thought that I could drag him to shore. He didn't want me to drown with him, so he let go of me and sank under the water. I know that's why he let go, so I could live. That's what hurt me the most.

As I grew older I met other friends. John MacAlese, Alec McCleish, and I were together day and night. When the war broke out we left school and joined the service in 1943, when we were seventeen. I got out in January 1946, and got a job on the railroad. There I made friends with Pat Mariano, Joe Sarro, and a few others, guys I'd known before a little bit. Once we worked together on the railroad we became close friends. We worked hard those days, moving 400-pound barrels. We were supposed to work two to a barrel, rolling them onto the freight car and stacking them upright, but I moved the barrels on my own. It was quicker that way. I could fill an entire car by myself and then take off for coffee on the sly. I knew the girls working in the cafeteria and I would talk to them.

I met my wife, Grace, at Pat Mariano's wedding in 1948. She was a bridesmaid, and I was an usher. When I met her, she was coupled up with another usher and I was coupled up with another bridesmaid. At the reception, I wanted to dance and talk only to Grace and not the girl I was supposed to be with. It caused an argument, but I didn't care. Then after that day, we started going steady and got married in 1950.

In 1958, the railroad company I worked for went out of business, and the jobs moved to New Haven, but I didn't want to move to New Haven. I was out of a job for one year, and I worked during that time for the State Department. I worked on the highway with college kids, who ran mad. They went off fishing and were running around, so I quit that job. A few months later I had the chance to go into business. My father-in-law lived four or five houses down from a store that was going out of business. He came to me and asked if I wanted to help him buy the place and run it and I said yes. That's why it's called Marascio's Market, first after my father-in-law and then after my wife.

I paid rent for the first ten years, then I bought the land next door in case I got evicted, so I could build my own store. I was paying rent to St. Anthony's Society. I decided I'd offer to buy it. At first they said yes, but then put an ad in the paper to see if they could get a better price. I offered another ten thousand dollars, and they jumped at it. I bought it, and I've had it for forty years. I've made so many friends through my business; many loyal customers have become friends. There's a group of us who go to breakfast every Sunday without fail—Joe Ciardi, Dennis D'Marzio, Richie Ferzoco, Carmen Filetti, and "Foota" Amatucci. They cut the grass for me in the summer and when there's snow, they come around and shovel. These are good friends, family friends, who go to each others' parties and help each other, but I haven't forgotten my mother. I still make sausages just the way she taught me, and they are the most popular item I sell.

Justice & Activism

SAVING MISSION HILL

Theresa Parks

I grew up in the Mission Hill Project in the 1940s when it consisted of brick buildings that were pleasant to look at and sturdily built, just like the people living there. My parents were Irish. Mother was born in Belmont, the youngest of six children. When she was very young, the whole family returned to County Galway, Ireland, where she remained until she was in her twenties. Dad was born in Ireland but met Ma in America. He worked for the railroad and was a quiet family man. We were not well-off, but thought we were the richest people in the world. Neighbors all knew each other and pitched in to help. When clothes were outgrown, they were sent to another family who could use them. If a neighbor asked you to go to the grocery store, you were happy to go. Money was never an issue; there wasn't any, so not to worry.

Mother was striking in appearance. She had perfect posture, always stood up straight, and walked tall. She had smooth porcelain skin, snow-white hair, and baby blue eyes that sparkled. She always wore a smile, had a great sense of humor, and never indulged in idle gossip about her neighbors. Instead, she spent her days helping people and teaching my sister Anna and me to do the same. From an early age, we were expected to assist other families by clearing off precious clothesline space, babysitting, or carrying bundles for women upstairs.

Once when Ma came home from work at Boston City Hospital, she asked me how I spent my day. Gladly, I shared that I'd helped a neighbor with small children by going to the store for her. Upon my return, she gave me a dime, which I proudly showed my mother. Ma immediately responded that I had to give it back. She explained that we helped people not for rewards but because we could. That was the end of that story and that dime, but it was Mother's attitude of helping that influenced me throughout my life.

I married Bob Parks who was from Jamaica Plain. He had been raised with values similar to mine, and we tried to instill the same attitude in our family. For years, when I worked at a dry cleaner in Mission Hill, the owner would give me any leftover clothing. With those clothes and other donations I received, I held flea markets to provide affordable clothing to my neighbors. I used the money to purchase turkeys and canned goods for needy families in Mission Hill and Jamaica Plain. These actions created bonds of community that came in handy one day when some Harvard medical students knocked at my door.

Up through the 1960s, Mission Hill was made up of mostly Irish Catholic families who attended the Mission Church. Families lived in two- and three-story wooden-framed houses built in the 1800s. Neighborhood children attended either Mission Grammar or the

Farragut School. Many couples met during Wednesday night no-
venas at Our Lady of Perpetual Help, went to dances at Hibernian
Hall, and eventually got married in the basilica. Whether living
on Huntington Avenue, Francis Street, or Fenwood Road, it was a
tightly knit community.

In the fall of 1968, Bob and I relocated to 52 Francis Street with our
four children. Three students showed up on our doorstep asking if
we had heard about Harvard's plans to build the biggest medical
institution in the country. Dean Ebert had announced to the papers
that houses would be torn down to make way for the university's
expansion. I hadn't heard the news and was shocked! We had just
moved and I knew that my mother, who lived with us, would not
want to leave the neighborhood. I asked the students several questions but they didn't know much more. I then said, "Well, I'm going to have to go out and organize." They asked, "Are you a community organizer?" I answered, "No, but I'll be whatever you want
me to be."

Mission Hill residents were unaware that between 1963 and 1968
Harvard had bought up many properties using "straws"—people
sent to the neighborhood to purchase homes deceptively. Home-
owners had been offered substantial incentives to sell their houses,
such as being allowed to live in them rent-free for up to one year after the sale. We were about to go up against the endowment of one
of the world's wealthiest institutions.

With students Doug Levinson and Jeanne Neville, I began going
door-to-door on Saturday afternoons to talk with neighbors about
what was happening in our community. I was the new person on the

block, but people recognized me from walking back and forth to the cleaners. As I informed residents about the issues, the students took notes about everyone we spoke with—their name, phone number, how long they had lived in Mission Hill, and any other facts that might be useful. Even though they were Harvard medical students themselves, Doug and Jeanne helped because they were also outraged by Harvard's plans.

As our organizing progressed and neighbors began to talk daily about the situation with Harvard, my husband Bob approached the Massachusetts Mental Health Center about getting meeting space. They let us use their chapel to hold a monthly meeting on Sundays. We followed Robert's Rules of Order and created a space for people to ask questions and state their concerns. Soon architect John Sharratt began to help us to identify who owned land in the community and to survey residents about the types of housing they desired. We also got a pro bono lawyer to incorporate our group; we called ourselves the Roxbury Tenants of Harvard (RTH).

Our next move was to get Dean Ebert to tour our neighborhood and see its deteriorating conditions. With plans to demolish the community, Harvard had neglected its housing stock and people were living with ceilings literally falling down on them. Despite Harvard's negligence as a landlord and threats of displacement, Dean Ebert found people who were resolved to stay in Mission Hill. The media began picking up on the struggle. I appeared on television several times talking about our fight to save Mission Hill. Harvard got the message when donations to its endowment began to drop off.

With pressure shifting onto the university, we handed Harvard a list of demands, including the need for a rental office dedicated to finding adequate replacement housing in Mission Hill for any residents displaced by Harvard's plans. We added an agreement that realtors had to rent to families over college students.

For many years, we went back and forth with the university, asserting our rights to live in Mission Hill and forcing them to be accountable to us about the development of their medical campus. Over time, we gained their respect and wore down their resolve to the point that we were seemingly working side-by-side to develop the neighborhood.

In 1976, we won a major battle and were allowed to plan and develop affordable housing on thirteen and a half acres of Harvard-owned land on Huntington Avenue and the Riverway, the site of the former House of the Good Shepherd convent. Roxbury Tenants of Harvard ultimately built Mission Park, a mixed-income community consisting of 775 units in a twenty-seven-story tower, three medium-rise buildings, and several modern townhouses. Bob became the organization's first executive director, and many Mission Hill families relocated there in the 1970s. Harvard's intention to take over our community had been successfully turned around so that it actually helped update our neighborhood and strengthen our community's bonds. In 1999, Harvard passed complete ownership of the Mission Park development over to RTH. Our victory was complete!

Since then, I've continued to live, work, and organize in Mission Hill. I work in the senior center at the Flynn House in Mission Park organizing activities, trips, bingo, and weekly chat meetings for seniors. I still pressure management from time to time to meet residents' needs and continue to hold flea markets to provide special treasures to my neighbors. Having taken part in the development of Mission Park was a great honor, and Bob and I loved every minute of the challenge. Residents there decided to name a building after us, the Robert and Theresa Parks Community Building.

WORKING FOR JUSTICE

EMBAJADORA A LOS MAYORES

Olga Dummott

Translated by Aaron Devine and Kathleen Olesky

Traducido por Aaron Devine y Kathleen Olesky

I have been involved in many community organizations since I came to the United States from Cuba in 1948. As a child, I remember running from my mother on Saturday mornings to go and help the elderly or the blind. I would always offer to help babysit little children so that their mothers could go shopping.

My father, Charles Henry Johnson, was born in Richmond, Virginia, and was the son of slaves. He was the first black Baptist missionary to come to Cuba. He arrived there in 1905. I was only five years old when he died, but I remember he was a perfect gentleman. My mother, Evalilian Dummott, was from Barbados in the West Indies. She moved to Brazil at the age of thirteen and to Cuba years later. My mother spoke five languages: Portuguese, Spanish, English, Dutch, and French. I learned my compassion for all people from her. It's hard for me to describe my mother. To her, there was no such thing as color, no such thing as race; she treated all people equally with the same humble attitude. She was such a lady! She always sat with her legs perfectly crossed at the ankles. In Cuba, when someone in trouble with the government or the law came knocking on our door, she always hid them under the bed. When the authorities came looking for them, she would say that she hadn't seen them. "This person is someone's son," she'd explain to me. "We have to protect him."

I learned this spirit from my mother. As a young child, I was often late to school because I had stopped to help a blind person find their way, or because I had encountered a neighbor with a baby and accompanied her to the store. My mother got angry when I did this since I was too much of a "free spirit." I also helped the poor neighborhood kids get free food from wealthier families. Finally, I was so out of control that my mother decided to send me and my sisters to a boarding school in Cuba run by the Salvation Army. I attended the school of three hundred children for two years. Missionaries ran the school on the island of Triconia, the immigration center where deportations occurred. My mother was a cook in the private home of the Salvation Army's Colonel Walker. He helped her get my sisters and me into the school. Many of the students were children of revolutionary officials. I learned discipline at the school. In the morning, we were awoken by a whistle and ordered to make our beds. When we left the school, we knew how to take care of ourselves. My mother visited us twice a week, once in the middle of the week and once on Sundays. I remember waiting for her to arrive with her bags of food.

My mother died in 1943. Before her death, I had paid for insurance for her funeral but ran out of money. I told the insurance man that I had no more money. The florist took back the wreath from her coffin. There were no flowers, there was no wreath, and I had no money. Then a prostitute named Dulce, who my mother had once helped, put a bucket of roses at the foot of my mother's coffin. I was a little shocked but realized my mother would have said, "Never look down on people. They are all the same." When my mother died, the whole red-light district came out because she never looked down on them because that was the kind of person she had been.

After my mother died, Dulce took me around the city to help with my grief and to keep me company. She showed me many parts of the city and when she dropped me off, she wouldn't come into my neighborhood so that people wouldn't think that I was associating with her. Once I asked her why she did the work she did. She said, "It is all I know. It puts bread in my mouth and it pays my bills."

When I was sixteen years old, I was hired to work as a nanny for a rich doctor from Havana named Dr. Orlando Sosa. I took care of his six-month-old baby. I went deep into the plantation country with the family where they raised sugar, yucca, and *frijoles* (beans). Their plantation was in the mountains. The sugar cane grew to be six feet tall. Once when I was walking through the cane fields, my shoe got stuck in the mud and I never got it out.

The family served me meals in the kitchen, but the plantation workers ate in a separate dining area, so I decided to sit with them. Dr. Sosa didn't like this one bit. He asked me, "What right do you have to sit with them?" I answered, "When I am on my time, I sit wherever I want and I am going to sit here." The doctor didn't like this because the other nannies didn't do this. I said to the plantation workers, "You work on the plantation, you give us food. Why should I tolerate his nonsense? I'm free!"

The plantation workers were so happy, and they called me Doña Olga. They said that no other nanny had ever treated them like equals. "You surely can't be from the city, Doña Olga, because you don't act like the others. They thought they were better than us." The plantation workers always came to my window in the mornings and called out, "Doña Olga, we have fresh cream from the cow for you.

Doña Olga, we have fresh orange juice for you." When I left, they gave me a flag that read *un recuerdo de Camaguey* ("a memento from Camaguey") and they walked with me through the town to bid me goodbye.

I came to the United States on May 30, 1948. My aunt had sent for me because she needed someone to take care of her rooming house. I will never forget the night I arrived in Miami, Florida. First, my suitcase got lost. I asked a Cuban man if he could help me find my suitcase, and he just looked at me and said, "Lady, I don't speak Spanish." I was shocked because a man of my own nationality rejected me. A black man helped me. He put me back on the bus and asked the bus driver to make sure I got my belongings. When I boarded the empty bus, a white lady came on. "What is she doing here?" she asked the bus driver. "I want to sit here." Even though I understood her, I said to her, "No speak English. Me Cuban." When I got off the bus, I went to the restroom. A black lady was cleaning the bathroom and when she saw me, she said, "Not here. You can't use this." I used it anyway, but realized that I wasn't in Cuba anymore—these people were rude.

When I arrived in Boston from Cuba, there were scarcely any Cubans here. My first job in the States was at the Bernant Woolen Company on Bickford Street in Jamaica Plain. I put wool onto yarn strings and made boxes for the yarn. The factory hired another minority, an African American girl. There was a little gang of Irish girls who worked there, one named Ann. She called the new girl a "nigger." I turned to her and I asked, "She has a name, doesn't she?" Ann came charging over and called me an awful profanity, so

I judo-punched her. When the factory whistle blew, my boss told me to clean down my machine. "You are terminated for hitting another worker for no reason," he said. I replied, "If you had said to me what she said, I would have hit you, too." "You're fired," he said.

After that, I became very ill with a heart murmur and spent one month at home. Then one of my friends, an Italian girl named Maria DeSimone, went to the boss. She told him that I was really a nice girl and that she had witnessed the whole incident. Maria told the boss that I had been provoked by the other girl and had had no choice. She said that I had been right. The boss brought me back. *"Tiene su trabajo,"* he said. "You still have your job." I went on to have other positions there, and they closed the department after I left because no one worked like I did.

I have spent the better part of my life working for others since I was nine years old; I am now eighty-one. I have opened my house in Roxbury to strangers as my mother did. I call it *La Casa de la Caridad,* a place where people in distress can stay until they get on their feet. In the 1980s, tens of thousands of refugees called Marielitos left the port of Mariel, Cuba. Many of them had been in prison or had mental health problems. I opened La Casa de la Caridad to them. They could stay ninety days, and I helped them find housing or jobs in factories.

In 1982, I moved back to Jamaica Plain where I had started. I worked at Curtis Hall as the senior coordinator for the elderly. I was the only Hispanic working with two hundred fifty Caucasians who welcomed me. There weren't any programs to bring Spanish-speaking and non—Spanish-speaking people together. I started senior trips that mixed different people together so they would get to know each other. We still have a lot of work to do in Jamaica Plain and the city of Boston.

Since 2003, I have been the volunteer coordinator and ambassador for seniors at large. Recently my daughter asked me, "Mami, isn't it time for you to retire?" I replied, "I will do all I can as long as I have life to help others in distress regardless of who they are. I will show my love for humanity."

My mother taught me to be humble, to be neat, and most of all to be nice to everyone. I feel strongly about whatever mission I am called to do, and I serve all people with dignity and respect, regardless of their nationality, religion, or color. I believe that we must share what we have gracefully — not with "what's in it for me" motives but "what's in it for all of us."

Desde que llegue a los Estados Unidos de Cuba en 1948, me he involucrado en varias organizaciones comunitarias. Recuerdo que cuando era niña, siempre me huía de mi madre los sábados para ayudar a los ancianos o los ciegos. Siempre ofrecía cuidar a los niños para que sus madres pudieran ir de compras.

Mi padre se llamaba Charles Henry Johnson. Era hijo de esclavos negros nacido en Richmond, Virginia. Fue el primer misionero baptista que vino a Cuba cuando llegó en el año 1905. Apenas yo tenía cinco años cuando falleció, pero aún recuerdo que era un perfecto caballero. Mi madre se llamaba Evalilian Dummott y provenía de la isla Barbados. Se mudó a Brasil cuando tenía 13 años y después se estableció en Cuba. Hablaba cinco idiomas: el portugués, el español, el ingles, el holandés, y el francés. Ella me enseñó tener compasión para toda la gente. Me cuesta describir mi madre. Según ella, no había ni color ni raza. Trataba a todas las personas con la misma humildad y respeto. ¡Cuán elegante era! Siempre se sentaba con las piernas cruzaditas por los tobillos. Recuerdo que cuando yo era niña en Cuba y tocaba a nuestra puerta un fugitivo, mi madre lo escondía debajo de la cama. Cuando vinieron las autoridades a buscarlo, ella les decía que no le había visto. "Esta persona es hijo de alguien," nos decía mi mama. "Y hay que protegerlo."

De mi madre aprendí este espíritu de servicio a la humanidad. Muchas veces yo llegaba tarde al colegio cuando era niña porque paraba a guiar los ciegos cruzando la calle. O a veces me encontraba con una vecina llevando su bebe y las acompañaba a la tienda.

Mi madre se enojaba conmigo y me regañaba porque yo tenía un "espíritu libre [y rebelde]." También me involucraba en conseguir comida de los ricos para los niños mas pobres. Entonces decidió mi madre inscribirme en un colegio de internos de 300 niños y niñas dirigida por misioneros del ejército de salvación . Dos años vivía y asistía clases en ese lugar. La escuela se situaba en la isla Triconia donde hacían las deportaciones. Mi madre trabajaba como cocinera en la casa de un oficial del ejército de salvación llamado el Coronel Walker y el hizo arregló la entrada de mis hermanas al colegio. Muchos de los niños allí eran hijos de oficiales en la revolución. Allí aprendí la disciplina. Siempre nos despertaban con un silbado y nos ordenaban hacer las camas. Cuando salimos de allí, fuimos muy independientes. Mi madre nos visitaba dos veces la semana — siempre los domingos y otra vez durante la semana. Recuerdo como esperaba que me trajera bolsitas de comida.

Murió mi madre en 1943. Yo había pagado el seguro para su funeral antes, pero se me había acabado el dinero. Le dije al hombre de seguros que no tenía con que pagarle. El florista iba a quitar la corona de flores. No había flores, ni corona, ni plata. Entonces una prostituta que se llamaba Dulce vino y dejó una rama de rosas en el ataúd. Me dijo que mi madre la había ayudado una vez. Me sorprendí pero después me di cuenta de que mi madre siempre me decía: "No tengas prejuicios; somos todos iguales." Cuando falleció mi madre todas las muchachas del distrito rojo vinieron a despedirla porque ella nunca las volteaba la vista y así era.

Luego Dulce me llevaba por todas partes de la ciudad para consolarme. Me enseñaba muchos lados y cuando me devolvía al vecindario donde yo vivía, ella nunca entró porque no quería la gente supiera que me asociaba con ella. Una vez la pregunté porque trabajaba de prostituta. Me dijo: "Es el único trabajo que conozco. Me da pan para comer y paga mis deudas."

Cuando tenía 16 años, un próspero médico de Habana, Orlando Sosa me contrató como niñera para su bebé de seis meses. Viajé con su familia al campo donde se encontraban plantaciones de caña de azúcar, yuca, y frijoles. La caña crecía hasta dos metros de altura y una vez, caminando por allí se me pegó un zapato en el lodo y no lo podía sacar nunca.

Cuando estaba allí la familia me servía la comida en la cocina. Pero los obreros de la plantación comieron aparte. Decidí a sentarme con ellos. Al doctor Sosa no le gustó esto. Me acercó y me dijo:

"¿Qué derecho tienes para sentarte con ellos?"

Yo le contesté: "En mi hora de comer, me siento donde quiera y voy a sentarme acá."

Al doctor no le gustó porque las otras niñeras no se habían comportado de esa manera. Se lo dije a los obreros:

"Ustedes son los que trabajan para darnos la comida. ¿Por qué yo debo tolerar estas reglas absurdas? Soy libre."

Se pusieron muy contentos los obreros y me llamaban "Doña Olga." Ninguna otra niñera les había tratado como seres iguales como yo había hecho.

"Seguro que no es de la ciudad, Doña Olga, porque no se porta como las demás. Ellas pensaron que fueron mejores que nosotros."

Cada mañana vinieron los obreros a mi ventanita a decir: "Doña Olga, hay crema fresca de la vaca para usted. Doña Olga, tenemos jugo de naranja recién hecho para usted." Cuando al final me fui del campo, me dieron una bandera que dijo: "un recuerdo de Camaguey" y me acompañaron al pueblo para despedirme.

En el 30 de Mayo del 1948, me vine a los Estados Unidos. Mi tía pidió que viniera porque le hacía falta alguien que cuidara su pensión en Roxbury. Nunca me olvidaré de la noche cuando llegué a Miami, Florida. Me acuerdo que perdí la maleta. Le pedí a un señor cubano si me pudiera ayudar a encontrarla. Solamente me miró y me dijo en ingles: "Señora, no hablo español." Me asusté porque mi propio paisano de mi misma nacionalidad me había rechazado.

Un caballero negro vino a ayudarme. Él me puso en el autobús y pidió al conductor que me ayudara a encontrar mi equipaje. Cuando, subí en el autobús, subió una señora blanca; todos los asientos estaban vacíos. Ella le dijo al conductor:

"¿Que hace aquella aquí? ¡Yo quisiera sentarme aquí!" Aún que yo le entendí, se le dije: *"No espeak English, me Cuban* [No hablo ingles, soy cubana]."

Cuando me baje del autobús, me fui a los servicios. Una mujer negra limpiaba los servicios y cuando me vió, me dijo: "No puedes entrar aquí. Tú no puedes usar estos servicios." A pesar de eso, yo los usé. Pero me di cuenta de que ya no estaba en Cuba. ¡Cómo era esta grosera!

Mi primer trabajo en los EEUU fue en la compañía de Bernant Woolen en la calle Bickford en Jamaica Plain. Yo doblaba la lana y la ponía en cajas. Habia otra empleada de color, una muchacha negra. Había tambien una ganga de irlandesas que trabaja allí, una de ellas se llamaba Ann. Ann le llamó a la nueva muchacha "nigger." Cuando yo oí esto, le dije a Ann: "Esta muchacha tiene un nombre, ¿no?"

Ann me acercó y empezó a llamarme varias palabrotas que trataban de mi madre. Yo la golpeé fuerte. Cuando silbó el timbre de la fábrica, entró el jefe y me dijo que limpiara mi máquina. "Tu estás terminada por golpear a otra empleada sin razón," me dijo.

Le dije al jefe: "Si hubiera oído lo que ella me dijo, usted le habría golpeado tambien."

"Véte," me dijo.

Después de eso, me puse enferma con una murmura del corazón y pasé un mes en casa. Luego, una amiga mía del trabajo, una italiana que se llamó Maria Desimone fue a hablar a mi jefe.

Ella le dijo que yo era una chica simpática y ella había visto todo el caso. Maria le dijo al jefe que la otra muchacha, Ann, me había provocado y yo no tenía otro remedio. María le dijo que yo era justificada en mi reacción. El jefe me entregué el trabajo. Yo continué en esta compañía en varios puestos. Cerraron el departamento cuando me fui porque "nadie trabajaba como Olga."

Cuando yo llegué de Cuba, casi no habían cubanos aquí. Por el mayor parte de mi vida, he trabajado por otros desde que tenía 9 años, y ahora tengo 81. He abierto mi casa a los extranjeros como hizo mi mamá. Mi casa se llamaba "La Casa de Caridad" ubicada en Roxbury. Es un lugar donde la gente perdida o pobre puede quedarse hasta se encuentren estabilidad. En los años '80s', miles de refugiados salieron de Mariel, Cuba — se llamaban los marielitos. Yo les abrí la Casa de Caridad a ellos; ellos podían quedarse tres meses y mientras yo les encontraban casas o trabajo en fábricas.

En 1982, me volví a Jamaica Plain donde yo había empezado.

Vine a trabajar en Curtis Hall como la coordinadora de servicios para la gente mayor. Fui la única latina trabajando con 250 americanos. No había programas para unir la gente de habla inglés y los latinoamericanos. Organicé viajes y actividades para mezclar todo tipo de gente para que se conocieran. Todavía, tenemos mucho que hacer en Jamaica Plain y en la ciudad de Boston.

Desde del ano 2003, he estado la coordinadora voluntaria y la embajadora para la gente mayor. Hace poco, me dijo mi hija:

"Mamá, ¿no piensas a retirarte?"

Yo la contesté: "Yo voy a hacer todo lo que pueda mientras que tenga vida para ayudar a los que necesiten, no importa quienes son, voy a mostrar mi amor por la humanidad."

Mi mamá me enseñó como ser humilde, sana, y sobre todo como tratar bien a todo el mundo. Siento una profunda misión de servir a la gente y tratarla con dignidad y respeto, no importa la religión, el color de piel ni la nacionalidad. Creo que debemos compartir lo que tenemos con gracia, no con el motivo de que "como puedo yo aprovecharme" pero como todos podemos avanzar.

URBAN RENEWAL: MY TWO LOST NEIGHBORHOODS

Gloria Ganno

This is the story of how two of my family's homes were taken by the City of Boston through eminent domain within twelve years. Eminent domain is a law stating that government entities can seize private property without the owner's consent, but the owner must be paid "due compensation." However, many people often complain that they aren't paid what their property is worth.

I lived in three different homes in the South End. Two of our three houses were taken by eminent domain. Our first home at 31 Harvard Street was taken by the city in 1944 because the hospital on the adjoining property wanted to expand. I was six years old and my family was comprised of my parents, my two brothers, Tom and Peter, and me.

Owned by my Lebanese grandparents, the house was a freestanding, four-story, four-family, red brick building with an unusually big front yard. Trees and several benches lined the wooden walkway leading to the sidewalk. I played in that front yard while my grandmother, who we called Situ, sat on a bench in the shade of a tree.

The cellar held a mysterious well covered with a large wooden board. My dad said that he had dropped a stone down the well and it had taken a long time to hit the water far below. My grandfather, who we called Jidu, spent his time in the cellar making *araq,* a Lebanese liquor, and other potent drinks. Although he drank his share and smoked all his life, Jidu lived in his apartment until he died at the age of one hundred three. The New England Medical Center covers that section of Harvard Street today.

We were adjacent to Chinatown and what was called Syrian Town, where the Chinese, Syrians, Armenians, and other ethnic groups peacefully coexisted. Some were immigrants and their dress and varying cultures added lots of old-world street life. When Syrians and other groups moved away in the 1950s, Chinatown expanded and the entire area became Chinatown.

We moved from Harvard Street in 1944 to a nearby section of the South End called the New York Streets. The streets were named after cities in New York state—Troy, Genessee, Rochester, Oswego, Decatur, and Seneca—because the Boston & Albany Railroad had a depot nearby whose trains traveled through those cities. Our third-floor apartment at 8 Florence Street was across from Our Lady of Pompeii Church, where I made my first communion and confirmation. From my window, I watched parishioners throwing

rice on couples who had just gotten married. Four Greek families lived in the building until we moved in and broke the pattern. My grandparents moved to Decatur Street, which was the next street over. I began first grade in a new dress and long pigtails at the Andrew School on Genessee Street. From grades four to eight, I attended the Abraham Lincoln School in Bay Village. My mom and dad both got jobs in clothing factories, and Mom also sang evenings in downtown nightclubs.

Florence Street was one block long between Harrison Avenue and Washington Street, where we heard the squealing wheels of the el trains snaking along the tracks to Dover Street Station. My mom and I made many lifelong friends on this sunny street with its four-story, red brick row houses. Mel King lived at Florence and Washington Streets, and later made history as the first black man to run for mayor of Boston.

Traffic was light, so we roller-skated on the street, played hop-scotch on the sidewalk, and played ball in an empty lot that once held three houses. The church owned the lots, and paved and maintained them. It was a miniature playground for us kids, and a place for the older boys to play a competitive game of handball against the brick wall at one end. With three missing buildings plus the church and rectory, there were fewer residences, so our street was less crowded than others. On hot summer nights, we played kick the can and hide-and-seek in the dark while our parents socialized on the stoops.

When my parents split up, my mom rented an apartment near Florence Street at 364 Harrison Avenue. They couldn't get along with each other so I felt it was a positive thing. Tillie, a nice Jewish lady with a heavy accent, owned the building comprised of twelve apartments and two commercial spaces on the ground floor. She was always cheerful and very proud that as a widow, she was able to be financially independent. Tillie's son, a doctor in Brookline, was always asking her to move there and couldn't understand her attachment to the neighborhood. However, she preferred to stay with her friends and her social life. In fact, there were a number of people who could afford to live elsewhere but lived in the New York Streets by preference.

Geoffries, the Italian bakery next door, emitted scrumptious aromas of Italian bread and cookies. The scents wafted up to our third-floor apartment, and we couldn't resist buying a hot loaf. They also sold imported Italian cold cuts and had big wheels of Italian cheeses. A Jewish bakery called Green Friedman's was on the next block. We bought bagels and pumpernickel and rye breads hot from the oven. There were stores that sold fruits and vegetables, meat and fish markets, and specialty stores catering to different ethnic groups. Girdis's Meat Market at the corner of Florence Street sold lamb exclusively. We never ate so well as when we lived in the New York Streets.

During the mid-1950s, residents of the New York Streets received the notice to move. The Boston Housing Authority (BHA, later replaced by the Boston Redevelopment Authority) was taking our homes by eminent domain, so Tillie moved to Brookline. Sadly, although she was living in a more upscale place, she was lonely and missed her friends and her old neighborhood life. The elderly were hit especially hard by all the upheaval.

When food stores in the New York Streets closed, it created hardship for the surrounding neighborhoods that shopped there. I read in the Boston Redevelopment Authority's records that they believed that the New York Streets were over-served with food markets. However, they didn't know much about our neighborhood and the people in the surrounding area who depended on those markets to buy food. The South End had no supermarkets, so everyone shopped in the small stores. When they were gone, people lost their local places to buy food.

Residents of the New York Streets were heartbroken to be kicked out of their homes. Just as in the better-documented West End taking, the city played dirty tricks to get us out. For example, they shut off all the streetlights at night so that you couldn't see your way home, especially on starless nights. It was a dangerous thing to do and anything could have happened. That tidbit of information isn't in the city's records. You had to experience it to know about what they did to us.

The BHA tried to place us in South Boston's Columbia Point Projects. It was a lonely place, set off by itself with no stores and little bus service. I told the BHA that I wanted to live in Bromley Park in Jamaica Plain where my friends had moved, and that I refused to live in Columbia Point. They became angry and wouldn't help us anymore, because I had the audacity to refuse to live there. If you were poor, you didn't get much respect from those people. Who were we to choose where we wanted to live after they had snatched our homes from us?

Everyone from our neighborhood was scattered throughout the city and suburbs. We rented an apartment at 34 Amory Street in Jamaica

Plain. However, my brother and I still returned to the South End to hang out, and so did our friends. Our Lady of Pompeii Church was razed, but our parish priest, Father Pitaro, held annual reunions for his parishioners until he died. He always maintained a soft place in his heart for that small, twenty-two-acre neighborhood. Our Jewish neighbors also attended these reunions so that they could see people from the old days. With Father Pitaro gone, parishioners continued the reunions until several years ago. For more than fifty years they had come together, but sadly there were no longer enough of them left to hold a reunion anymore.

The Syrians from Syrian Town used to hold a huge event every year at the Chateau DeVille, which held several hundred people. They served a family-style roast beef dinner on large platters that kept coming if you asked for more. They also featured a twenty-piece American orchestra for regular dancing and a Syrian orchestra for line dancing. The event sold out quickly so you had to buy your tickets early, and what a time that was! That event is no longer held, but people from different parts of the South End still hold reunions today.

As teens, we used to walk or take the T all over the place. We even had a bus at the Broadway Bridge that took us to South Boston's City Point and Carson beaches. Being city kids, we could go almost anywhere on our own. Today, parents are always driving their kids somewhere in their cars. Imagine the luxury of having kids with no rides needed.

It's important to note that urban renewal didn't stop with the New York Streets. We were the first neighborhood to be razed, but during the urban renewal craze of the fifties, sixties, and seventies, the

South End lost 25 percent of its buildings. Residents who chose to stay in the South End were forced to move from place to place as the city took more properties. People began to fight back to keep the destruction from continuing and fortunately they succeeded.

Today, the South End's bow-front brick buildings are cherished rather than distained, and are part of the National Trust for Historic Preservation. The district contains the largest intact Victorian urban area in the nation. These architectural treasures are what our city would have lost if urban renewal had continued unchecked.

Although ugly commercial buildings replaced the New York Streets more than fifty years ago, at least people like me are still around to write the story of a time and place where many nationalities and ethnicities lived together peacefully.

LOOKING BACK ON BUSING

Francesca Johnnene

My Italian-born mother always said, "Pay attention, things change. Nothing lasts forever." I didn't understand the full meaning of her words until forced busing came to Boston in 1974.

I was raised in a tight-knit community and I wanted the same for my kids. So when I found myself a single parent, solely responsible for supporting my three young children, I moved back to my childhood neighborhood of Readville, near Hyde Park. My children started second, third, and fourth grades at the neighborhood grammar school. They walked to school with other children, often accompanied by a parent of a little one just starting school. The kids played together after school and had the opportunity to make friendships that could last a lifetime. Sometimes the kids were even able to come home for lunch. I was a working single parent and when my kids got sick at school, I could call a neighbor to pick them up. It was working out just as I had prayed it would. Then the bomb hit. A federal judge ordered the Boston Public Schools to institute forced busing so that our kids would be "integrated."

Boston neighborhoods were divided into busing areas called geocodes, and every parent received notice by mail outlining their new schools and geocodes. My children were to be separated and sent to three different schools in three different geocodes, one over eight miles away in Dorchester. I did not own a car. What if my kids got sick or hurt, missed a bus, or simply forgot their lunch? Three different schools, three different areas of Boston, and me with no car, no choice, no exception, and no appeal!

Before that judge forced busing on me, I had worked in my neighborhood and throughout Boston in programs like SummerThing, which was a family program that brought the arts and cultural and educational programs to all of Boston's neighborhoods. I met many people representing the varied ethnic and racial makeup of Boston's melting pot, so it seemed natural when I began to receive calls from parents in different neighborhoods asking what could be done to keep their kids close to home. Some parents cried and some swore, but all were upset. Hardworking families of different immigrant groups — Italian, Greek, Jewish, Polish, Armenian, Irish, Chinese, German — in various neighborhoods were the backbone of the city, working as homemakers, factory workers, teachers, firefighters, garbage men, electricians, policemen, doctors, and lawyers. They all shared the same feelings. They were hurt, fearful, and had a sense that their basic rights as parents were being taken away.

When I was asked to get involved, I did. Wouldn't you? I defended the parents, talked to lawyers and politicians, and learned a lot about our legal and political systems. I received invitations to speak in other locations including Dallas, Denver, and Kentucky. I quickly learned that forced busing would have a unique impact on Boston. In Dallas, we were picked up at the airport and after fifteen miles, I asked, "How much farther?" "Down the road," they answered. "Down the road" was another twenty miles or so. You see, Dallas already used buses to get their kids to school because of the greater distances. The concept of neighborhoods and the cultural identity it gave the children in Dallas wasn't as strong as in Boston. Forced busing would change Boston in ways that could not be compared with any other city.

I became a founding member of a group called ROAR (Restore Our Alienated Rights). It was a place for parents to join together to brainstorm, organize, lobby, and — yes — protest. At the start of meetings, people were asked to look around and see if there were any new faces. New attendees were asked to introduce themselves. Federal agents, state government agents, and reporters often attended. They were never asked to leave. Despite those who vilified us and called us names, ROAR's goal was to tell the truth of the effects busing had on our children, our families, our neighborhoods, and us. Looking back, you could say ROAR was a forerunner of the grassroots organizations used today to protect or advance a common cause. In our case, our common cause was to defend our rights as parents to decide where to live and where our children attended school.

During this time, I also served as president of my local Home and School Association (a cross between a PTA and neighborhood group). At the time every school had one. As president, I ran meetings, often attended by three to four hundred people, outlining how forced busing worked, what the geocode map meant, and how parents could get information about the different schools and neighborhoods their kids were being bused to. Instead of using pushpins on the map, I used diaper pins. These were babies, our babies, and I didn't want anyone to forget that.

I was not alone. Across the city, in all nineteen neighborhoods, people started getting involved, attending city council meetings, and opening information centers where parents could vent as well as get help and information. The disappointment and helplessness that we all felt found a voice. Some people forged strong bonds that would last a lifetime, including me.

A small group of parents from those years still meet on New Year's Day at my house. We remember the motorcades to Judge W. Arthur Garrity's home in Wellesley so he could see the real people impacted by his decision, not just a political ideology. We remember the meetings in the State House with Senator Joe Timilty and Representative Mel King, and their shared concern for the safety of the children and the impact busing would have on them. We reminisce about the stories from the policemen who had to control crowds in all sections of the city, patrol the schools, and monitor metal detectors. We remember the pain, fright, actions, reactions, and civil upheaval that we all saw and that remain with us today. We talk about our children and how much their lives changed — both for good and bad — from what we had hoped as a result of those times.

Huge changes were thrust on all of us. I often think of the mother that the police found wandering Hyde Park Avenue, dazed, shocked, and alone, with three pieces of paper in her hand — each one a different geocode notice, like those I had received, forcibly busing her kids to three different schools. She did not understand. How? How could this happen? After her local information center asked me to talk to her, I tried to explain, but what could I really say? That things change? Would it really be all right for her or her kids?

Judge Garrity's decision to order forced busing changed Boston and the lives of its people. We cried and fought. Husbands and wives divorced from the strain. Friendships were forged and others destroyed. Families crumbled and neighborhoods changed forever as close-knit, multigenerational, ethnic enclaves were torn apart when younger members moved away to other towns so that their kids could still walk to school. Was it worth it? Was the havoc wrought on Boston's schools, Boston's neighborhoods and families, and an entire generation of students even necessary?

My own family integrated fine without the interference of a court order. Before she died last year, my mother looked around our holiday dinner and reminded us, "I came from Italy and Dad was born here, but many types of Americans—Italian, Polish, Irish, Jewish, and Black—are all present around our dinner table."

Looking back, forced busing is gone and its success or failure is still under debate, but my family is still here—together, yet diverse—united by the love and joy we share with each other. My mother was right—things do change, most successfully when just left to do so on their own.

A Better Life

SOME DREAMS DO COME TRUE

Gwendolyn Keith

When I was a young girl of seven or eight, I wanted to be a nurse. I finally became one at age fifty-five.

When I came of age in 1934, I applied to Good Shepherd, a local nursing school, but they told me they were not taking colored students. Then they said that if I could find a roommate, they would accept me. Of course, my mother told me I had to do other work to pay the bills; I couldn't just go to school. That work went on and on, and I didn't end up going to nursing school. During the day, I worked in Newton cleaning and babysitting. I got married in 1940. My husband was a cook in the navy.

After we married, we moved into a one-room apartment in Boston. It had a bed, a bureau, and a bathroom. He heard about a one-bedroom apartment nearby, and when we moved in we didn't have a kitchen table. I was still commuting to Newton for day work when a friend's wife got me a job making men's clothing. I worked there ten years. Three of us stood on the line, doing the same work. One woman who did piecework had been there nineteen years; she was the oldest on the line. The company was going to let her go, but since I had a husband and could scramble, I left instead. They had a going away party for me and someone gave me a card that read, "With God, all things are possible." When times got tough over the years, I reflected on that saying.

I collected unemployment for a while and one day while I was meeting with my caseworker, I learned that I could be retrained for another job. She made a long list of careers I could train for, and one of them was to be a nurse (LPN). I got in under the Manpower Development Act. I was in my fifties when I started nursing school at the Trade High School for Girls in the late 1960s.

We took classes and worked shifts at Boston City Hospital for our practicum. I had both black and white patients. The nursing staff was also integrated. At the beginning, our instructor introduced us to the patients and explained what we were there to do. "This is Nurse Keith and if you have any problem with her, let me know."

I still use some of the things the head nurse, Miss Allen, taught me. You didn't call her *Mrs.* She was *Miss* Allen. She was a little spitfire—a short woman, black, and very strict. She worked Dowling 4 North (north was the women; south was the men).

Metal containers held sterile items. We put a cotton ball in with items to be sent to sterilization. The containers came back with the top on tight, marked "sterile." One day Miss Allen caught me. I had opened one and set the lid on the counter. "Young lady!" she said. (She called all of us "young lady.") "You just made a mistake. What did you do?"

I went through my steps, and then I remembered. If I set the lid on the counter lip-side down, it would no longer be sterile. She made me practice twenty to thirty times taking a top off, flipping it over, and putting it down. I still open my peanut butter jars that same way today.

Miss Allen's floor was just so. Her floor never had infections. The patients were organized four to a quadrant with a curtain dividing them. The curtains were just so, not an inch off. After you gave a patient a bath, Miss Allen would check behind their ears, between their toes, and in their belly button. Woe be to you if she found anything wrong.

I was cold at work so one day I brought a white sweater to wear with my uniform. The first day I wore it, Miss Allen stopped me. "Young lady, we don't wear sweaters," she said. "But, Miss Allen," I replied, "I'm cold." "Oh, you're cold?" she asked. "Yes, ma'am," I said. "Take the sweater off, and I'm going to make sure you stay warm." And she did. She gave me extra work and I was running the whole day.

I graduated in 1971 and was the oldest in the group at age fifty-five. After I graduated, my friend was after me for my test results, but I couldn't bring myself to open the letter. Finally, I let her open it. The top score was 500 and I had earned 495! My instructor, Mrs. Manassin, asked what I was going to do next. I said I wanted to take a couple weeks off and then look for a job. She wrote a letter, put it in an envelope, and said, "Take this to the nursing director's office; she's expecting you." The nursing director was a member of my church; our daughters were friends. I went to see her after a short break and she hired me. At first, I floated between departments and floors. Floating was murder because everyone had a different way of doing things, but I learned. Later, I moved to the fourth floor and worked with female patients.

My first day as a nurse, I was assigned to four patients under head nurse Mary Howard. My first patient had pneumonia and I had to give her a bed bath. While I was bathing her, she intentionally coughed and spit on me more than once. When I finished I reported to my head nurse, but she didn't say anything.

The second patient gave herself a bath, but she couldn't wash her feet, so I grabbed a little plastic tub and washed her feet in that. We talked about how clean feet make you feel good and had a good laugh.

My third patient had just been diagnosed as diabetic. Although we had talked about it in school, I didn't know enough about it to give her any advice. At lunchtime, I picked up some pamphlets for her to read and some for me as well.

The fourth man was an alcoholic. He came in regularly, all banged up. He had cuts and bruises all over that hurt when I washed and dried him. I applied ointment and sent him on his way. I told him if he came back again, I was going to have the man from Pine Street Shelter come in to see him. One day, a woman came to visit him and I later asked him about her. He said that she was his wife. I told him that if he kept on drinking, she might leave him one day. After that, I didn't see him for about three months. As I was leaving work one day, I heard a voice say, "That's her," and saw a man pointing at me. I barely recognized him. His wife came up to me and thanked me.

She told me he had stopped getting drunk and was working every day. Remembering what I had said to him, it made me feel good.

I worked at Boston City Hospital for ten years. I had to retire from nursing after my bypass surgery when I was sixty-seven, but it felt good to help people and feel useful. My dream of becoming a nurse had finally come true. With God, all things really *are* possible.

MISS FACEY

Gladys Facey

My grandchildren are my life to me. It's my duty to raise them to be the best that they can be in whatever they try their hand at. This was how I was raised.

I was born on March 24, 1922. I never knew my mother, Elizabeth, because she died in childbirth. I do have her high school graduation picture. My father, James, was a good, fun-loving man. My paternal grandmother in Somerville, who I called Ma, raised me. I was her baby and felt that I had all of her love and care. When I die and go to heaven, the first thing that I'm going to do is look for her.

Country life in Somerville was good for the Chute family. If there were any problems, I never knew about them. Of course, there were money issues — this was during the Depression — but we all pitched in. My first paying job was helping an elderly woman in Arlington bake perfect cakes, as her hands were full of pain. Each day after school, under her watchful eye, I mixed the ingredients for these perfect cakes in a big mixing bowl. There was no such thing as an electric mixer. It was fun and I was paid five dollars per week.

I was thirteen years old and felt rich. My earned money went toward the house expenses, just like everyone else's, and that felt so good.

When I turned sixteen, I started spending days at a time with my maternal grandparents in Boston. The Bowles were members of the Black Bostonian high society. My grandfather—I called him Sugar—was the bandleader for the well-known Bowles Black and White Orchestra. My uncle, George Francis Bowles, had graduated from MIT and his college friends were always around. My grandmother, Edith, was a social butterfly known for her piano playing. She gave very popular social gatherings at their home near the corner of Massachusetts and Columbus avenues. She never called me by my first name, Gladys. She thought that it was too common and represented my father's side of the family. She called me by my middle name, Elizabeth, instead. Thus began my two years of living in two very different worlds—the homespun country life of Somerville and the high-society, hoity-toity life of the Bowles of Boston.

As the only child, I was spoiled, especially by my grandfather Sugar and Uncle Francis. I went to them for whatever I wanted. I never went to my grandmothers because they were very strict. Neither of them gave in to my requests, one out of love and the other out of a little jealousy. I had very fancy clothes for Grandma Edith's high-society gatherings of Black intellectuals, musicians, and business owners in Boston. I had to speak differently; everything was very proper. Afterward, I took a taxi up Massachusetts Avenue to Somerville and the country living and kitchen of Ma, where she made scrumptious meals and never allowed anyone to cook on her potbellied stove. I learned so much about life in those two worlds, but I wish that I had paid a little more attention.

On April 10, 1940, William Facey and I were married by a justice of the peace. I was eighteen and we eloped. We tried to hide it for a while but failed miserably because his mother came to Ma's house and demanded to know why they had not been introduced. When the dust finally settled down, so did we, in Somerville. We had our first child, James, two years later and our daughter, Sandra, a year and a half after that.

Our life was normal. That is to say, there were good times and there were bad times. We had Ma Chute and Daddy to help us. I had been married for fifteen years when I heard about the new housing expansion called Bromley Heath in Jamaica Plain. I was determined to move my family into one of those new apartments. I filled out the application and when I didn't get a response, I took the children with me to the housing offices every day for two weeks until I received an apartment. It was 1956 and Bromley Heath had been open for less than two years. Everything was new and that's where I started a life as Bromley Heath's most popular babysitter.

It started with one little girl who I kept overnight because her mother worked nights. When her mother started working two jobs, it was easier to keep her five days a week. Some people saw me with a child who wasn't mine, and they asked, "Are you babysitting?" I said, "Yes," and they asked, "Would you babysit my child from this time or that time?" I started charging two dollars a day. For two dollars a day, I worked five days a week, which meant ten dollars a week. Half the time, I didn't get paid the two dollars a day or the ten dollars a week, but it didn't matter. I babysat. By the time I stopped babysitting thirty years later, I had taken care of two generations of the same family, up to twenty or twenty-five children at a time. I adopted one of them. We marched down the street to get the bus and went on field trips. Everybody knew us. They called me Miss Facey.

During that time my husband died, and my son helped me through that despair. I have my husband's ashes in a drawer and when I go, he will be buried with me. That was his wish.

There is nothing more difficult than burying your children. I have had to bury my daughter and my son. Sandra died from breast cancer. My son died in Kingston, Jamaica, and we have never been able to find out how or why, which makes it hurt even more.

Before Sandra died, she said, "Mom, please take good care of my children for me and do your very best for them." I think that's what I've done. I kept the oldest, Dawn, in private school. Couldn't afford to, but I did it anyway. From Boston Latin, she went to Wellesley College. She did this on her own. From there, she went to Harvard, where she graduated with a Doctorate of Law. Tremana is in her last year of college and the youngest, Armani, is a senior in high school. They're all doing so well. I figure that I have paid my dues to my daughter and to anybody else. I raised them in a project that everybody said was so bad. I have given them my life, love, and time. I thank God for giving them to me.

Now, I'm in the calm, quiet phase of my life. Not that I am ready to die; I just do what I want. I'm still very busy with elder activities and outings. I go shopping for friends and family. If there's something I want to do, I take my time and do it. At eighty-seven, that's good. No cane, nothing. I have learned to say what is on my mind, and never let anything fester. My grandkids will tell you, "[If] Grandma don't like something, she's going to tell you." After that, it all depends on how you take it. On the flip side, I am always looking for new ways and things. You're never too old to learn something new. I'm planning to be a hundred years old, then I'll slow down. My motto is "Be happy, don't look back. Everything good is ahead." Love.

MY JOURNEY
TO JAMAICA PLAIN

Gail Cowgill

My first job was setting our family table. Every time I had a birthday, my mother told me that I had more chores to do — make beds, do dishes, hang clothes on the line, mind babies, and on and on. When I was around thirteen or fourteen, I started minding other people's babies and making a little money.

I was born and brought up in the blue-collar mill town of Lowell, Massachusetts. After coming home from World War II, my dad worked at Suffolk Knitting for the rest of his life, never earning much more than minimum wage. My mother raised five kids, and I was the oldest. The only career direction I ever received from my parents was my father saying, "You can't go to the mill."

It seems like I've tried every other way to make a living. I've worked in advertising and law offices, been a cocktail waitress, run an antique shop and a bed-and-breakfast, and worked many temp jobs.

My parents moved to Derry, New Hampshire, after I graduated from high school. There were very few jobs there. I used to go to auctions, flea markets, and the dump for fun. I collected antiques and housewares, everything on the cheap. It was hard to meet new friends in a new town. I was working at Raytheon in Andover, Massachusetts, and met a girl named Nancy who had moved from Weston. Nancy gave me the idea of moving to Boston.

I told my parents that I would get a job in Boston and then move there. They just looked at me like I was crazy. I secretly went to the Boston Unemployment Office and they sent me out on interviews. The Bresnick Company hired me as a clerk in the media department. I was so naïve that I did not even understand what advertising was or what I would be doing. When I got home and told my parents, they were stunned. They were angry about losing the money I gave them for room and board. Dad told me they would lose the car if I left. Being the good kid that I was, I paid them fifty dollars a month for the next two years even though I was also renting a room at the YMCA on Berkeley Street. It was very hard, but I was used to not having much money.

This was 1962 and I was twenty years old. Bresnick was the largest advertising agency in Boston at the time. Through my job I went to all the major parties and openings in town—the opera house, all the theatres, and the flower show. The opening of Faneuil Hall was absolutely unbelievable, with popular bands, celebrities, news personalities, and wine flowing with every course of the meal.

After more than ten years in advertising, I wanted a change, but the other fields I tried didn't work out for me. It seemed that I was always the one being let go. From losing job after job and always being poor, I learned to be frugal. Everything I owned was old and used when I bought it: my furniture, dishes, and glasses. I purchased my bed on the side of the road for five dollars.

I was living in Brighton when I found myself unemployed once again at thirty-three. There was an old barbershop across the street that had closed, and I thought maybe I could open an antique shop. I found out that my landlord owned the space and he agreed to let me rent it. I got busy painting and cleaning, got my business license, and opened my antique shop, called Poppy's. I didn't even need to buy any stock because I had collected so many antiques over the years. At the time I was also exercising my green thumb and growing annual flowers from seed — geraniums and coleus — so I sold those too.

When my brother came to visit from the Cape, he said I should open a shop down there. It was 1976, and I moved Poppy's to Provincetown. The shop did good business, but I discovered that you really need a partner or money to keep a shop going — so I went back to Brighton and temp jobs.

In 1980, I had been living in my Brighton apartment for twelve years when my friend Jane and I decided to share an apartment downtown. We moved to Tremont on the Common, into a lovely, nineteenth-floor, two-bedroom apartment. We loved entertaining; I cooked a lot and Jane thought I was really good at it. One day she read about the Johnson & Wales Culinary Art School in Providence, Rhode Island, and suggested that I sign up for the weekend program. I told her she was crazy, but I kept thinking about it and finally applied to the program. I worked full-time during the week and attended J&W every weekend. After a year, I moved to Brookline and attended a culinary school in Cambridge, where I graduated in 1984.

After graduation from culinary school, I worked through temp agencies as a legal secretary and cooked on weekends at a retirement home in Jamaica Plain. I enjoyed working as a cook, but the jobs didn't pay well enough to do it full-time. Sometimes I worked for a caterer at private parties in Cambridge, Newton, and Boston. It was different from office work, and I liked exploring different foods and wines. Living in Brookline made it difficult to have a car, and without a car my catering was limited to local events.

I began working as an executive secretary at Gerber Childrenswear and catered some of their executive meetings, but the company ended up relocating down south and I lost my job. Around this same time, my roommate decided to move out. I was in my late forties and could not conceive of getting a new roommate.

Gail with her antiques

While I was collecting unemployment, I needed to keep busy so I started painting my apartment, putting up wallpaper, redoing the hardwood floors—anything to make the apartment look good. I taught myself how to do everything. After all of my hard work, my apartment was in mint condition.

Somehow, I got the idea that I should open a bed-and-breakfast. It seemed like a natural fit for me, and Brookline was the perfect location since it had public transportation and was close to a number of colleges. From my early work experiences in advertising, I knew Boston very well and could direct my guests anywhere they wanted to go. I kept brochures and gave them ideas and information about all the hot spots.

My apartment was filled with all the antiques I had collected over the years, plus my homemade curtains and bedspreads. I prepared big breakfasts and lots of homemade goodies. I loved having guests. People from all over the world stayed with me: professors from other countries, an elderly couple who lived next door to a farm where ingredients for Gerber baby food were grown, and a writer who wrote a story about her stay with me. I was so busy with guests that I moved out of my bedroom and into my dining room so that I could rent two rooms. My guests really enjoyed themselves and many sent me thank-you notes and gifts. I ran my B&B for three years.

By 1993 I was working at a large law firm, making a good salary, and still running my B&B. Single women had started buying condos and homes, and I got the idea that maybe I could, too. Real estate was reasonable and interest rates were low. For a few months I looked at condos in Brookline and could not find one I liked or could afford. A friend suggested I look in Jamaica Plain, and that's where I found my condo. I became a homeowner! I can't tell you how happy this made me.

I now feel like I'm part of a warm community with lots of lovely small children who give me smiles and hugs. I live on a corner plot and spend lots of time on my front porch. I have a garden at my home and a plot in a community garden where I also plant a large area of common space with flowers. I grow my own herbs and vegetables and freeze them for the winter. I'm very happy to be a homeowner in such a nice neighborhood.

"SEWING" THE SEEDS OF A BETTER LIFE

"SEMBRANDO" LAS SEMILLAS DE UNA VIDA MEJOR

Elsa Nin

Translated by Kathleen Olesky

Traducido por Kathleen Olesky

My name is Elsa Nin and I am from the Dominican Republic, born in the city of Barahona on May 15, 1936. I arrived in this country in 1967 with much hope of advancing economically because my family was very poor.

My mother was a very good wife to my father. She had eight children. Two of them eventually died, three came to the United States, and the others remained in the Dominican Republic with my parents. Neither my father nor mother ever came to visit the U.S. My family were country people and quite strict. When I was young, about twelve years old, my older sister wanted to cut my hair. I didn't want her to because my parents didn't want us to cut our hair. There was a saying that when a girl wants to cut her hair, it means she wants to get married, and we were too young to get married. My sister insisted that I cut her hair and that she cut mine. Afterwards we showed our mother and she really scolded us. My father just didn't say anything.

A few days later, the lady who did the laundry in our house asked me why I didn't wear earrings. I said we didn't wear them because we didn't have pierced ears. Then, out of sight of my mother, she dared to pierce my ears and put earrings that were called sleepers in my ears. I showed my mother and she said it was all right.

As it turns out, I did marry very young—at age seventeen—and I had four children. That marriage lasted thirteen years. When my second husband fell in love with me, the first thing he told me was that he had permanent residency in the U.S. and he wanted to bring me. I said no because I didn't know anything about this country. He begged me so many times that, after six months, I finally agreed. He had an apartment on Dudley Street. Even though there weren't many Latinos here at that time, I really liked Boston.

Work has always been very, very important to me and I have had the good fortune to always work. I arrived in the U.S. on a Saturday and I started work the very next Monday. I had worked as a seamstress in a shirt factory in the Dominican Republic, so I came here with a skill.

I was twenty-nine years old when I immigrated, and I had to leave my four children behind in my country. They ranged in age from nine to seventeen. My mother took care of them. I suffered and cried a lot for them. I endured four years without them, but I obtained residency for them as soon as I could because I wanted them here with me.

At the beginning, my husband worked with me in a curtain factory where I sewed. Finally, my children came. My oldest daughter worked together with me as a seamstress, my son got a job as a mechanic, and the other children went to school. I have always worked really hard to provide everything for my children. My husband and I eventually separated and I was alone, fighting hard to get by. I moved from Dudley Street to Jamaica Plain. Although it was difficult supporting my children alone, I always felt happy when I was working. I also worked in a sweater factory owned by Cubans, but then I established myself as an expert in making curtains. Even now, I make curtains, bedspreads—everything for my house, my family, and my friends.

My work as a seamstress involved preparing the fabric before I gave it to the upholsterer who then finished the piece of furniture. The company was called Décor on Harrison Avenue. I was the only Latina in the company. I was able to learn a little English from my boss and my coworkers who always talked to me and I tried to understand them. During my lunch hour, I studied English.

I didn't want to retire but, at my age, I felt very tired. My coworkers encouraged me to keep working, but I couldn't continue even though I wanted to. I came to my decision and told my boss who said I would be missed. He was very kind to his employees, and I was accustomed to working with him and the others. It was not easy to leave after so many years of working, but I was able to receive Social Security and I feel very fortunate, thank God.

After so many years of struggling for my family, all of them have turned out well. My children are married and have good careers and homes of their own, and my grandchildren have graduated from college. I am grateful for the opportunities that I have had in this country so that I could advance my family.

Mi nombre es Elsa Nin y soy dominicana, nacida en la ciudad de Barahona el 15 de mayo del año 1936. Llegué a este país en el año 1967 con mucha esperanza de progresar porque mi familia era muy pobre.

Mi mamá era una esposa muy buena con mi papá. Tuvo ocho hijos y después de muchos años fallecieron dos de ellos, tres vinieron aquí y los otros se quedaron en la Republica Dominicana. Ni mi mamá ni mi papá me han visitado aquí nunca. Mi familia era gente campesina y muy estricta. Me recuerdo cuando yo era pequeña, a los doce años de edad, mi hermana mayor me dijo que quería cortarme el pelo. Yo no quería porque mis padres no querían que lo cortara. Se dice que la muchacha que quiere cortarse el pelo quiere casarse y nosotros éramos muy pequeñas. Pero mi hermana insistió que yo le cortara el pelo y ella me cortó el mío. Luego fuimos a donde estaba mamá y ella nos regañó. Mi papá no nos dijo nada. Al cabo de unos días me preguntó la señora que lavaba la ropa de mi casa que porque no nos dejaban usar aretes. Yo le dije no tenemos como usarlos que necesitamos un hoyito en la oreja. Pues, escondida de mami, la señora se atrevió hacerme el hoyito y puso unos aretes que se llaman dormilones y luego mi mamá dijo que estaba bien.

Resultó que me casé muy jovencita, a las 17 años y tuve cuatro hijos. Este matrimonio duró trece años. Cuando mi segundo esposo se enamoró de mí, la primera cosa que me djio que quería traerme a este país. Yo le dije que no porque yo no conocía nada de este país pero el me rogaba mucho y después de seis meses, me vine. El tenía un apartamento en la calle Dudley. No había muchos hispanos en aquella época pero me gustó mucho el país.

El trabajo siempre ha sido muy importante para mí y siempre he tenido la suerte de trabajar. Llegué un sábado y empecé a trabajar el próximo lunes. Trabajaba en una fábrica de camisas en mi país entonces llegué aquí con este talento. Yo vine a los 29 años; tuve que dejar mis cuatros hijos en mi país. Ellos tenían 9 a 17 años. Mi mamá los cuidaba. Yo sufría y lloraba mucho por ellos. Duré cuatro años aquí sin ellos. Yo solicité la residencia por ellos en seguida porque los querían aquí conmigo.

Mi esposo trabajaba conmigo en una fábrica de cortinas. Yo me quedé cociendo. Por fin, mis hijos vinieron. Mi hija mayor trabajaba conmigo en costura. Mi hijo consiguió trabajo como mecánico. Los otros fueron a la escuela. Yo siempre trabajaba duro para comprar cosas para mis hijos. Mi esposo y yo nos separamos y yo tenía que estar trabajando sola. Aunque fue duro, siempre me sentaba feliz cuando estaba trabajando. Yo cocí suéteres también en una fábrica cubana y me establecí en cortinas. Yo hago cortinas, cubrecamas, de todo para mi casa y para mis amigas.

Voy a contar la historia de mi último trabajo que fue el último para mi retiro. Lamentaba mucho retirarme pero a mi edad me sentía muy cansada. Mis compañeros me daban mucho ánimo para seguir trabajando pero no podía continuar por mi edad a pesar de que yo quería seguir trabajando. Era el día de mi decisión, el jefe me dijo que ellos iban a extrañarme. Él fue una persona muy amable con sus empleados y así me fui acostumbrando, cosa que no era fácil después de tantos años de trabajo. Luego el seguro social me ha recompensado y me he sentido muy bien, gracias a Dios.

Mi trabajo era coser, preparar el forro del mueble para entregárselo al tapicero para que él terminara el mueble. El nombre de la compañía era Décor en la avenida Harrison. Yo siempre era la única latina. Yo pude aprender un poco de inglés con mi jefe y los empleados compañeros que me hablaban y yo siempre trataba de entender. Y estudiaba el inglés durante la hora del almuerzo.

Después de tantos años de luchar por mi familia, todos salieron bien. Mis hijos están casados y tienen sus propias casas y mis nietos se graduaron de universidades aquí. Yo agradezco las oportunidades que he tenido en este país para avanzar con mi familia.

Beams of Light

THE AUNT WHO SPOILED ME

Ann Labbe

My mother, Beatrice Downey, came to America in 1927 on what she always said was "the last boat from Ireland." She had gone to school until fifth or sixth grade, and after that had been working on the farm. Her mother told her to join her brother Willie and her sister Margaret in America because there was nothing for her to do in Ireland. She said, "Go and better yourself."

Willie had come to Boston first, then he sponsored Margaret, who in turn sponsored Beatrice. My mother was very eager to see Willie and Margaret, who had left Ireland more than a year before. She wrote them a letter with the date and time of her arrival in East Boston.

Mom used to tell me that she arrived in the U.S. with just the clothes on her back. I imagine her lonely and lost on that boat, a seasick and terrified eighteen-year-old. I picture her in a long black skirt, a simple blouse, and a coat, with a small bag carrying only her passport and entry papers. She was on the boat for a week and sick for the whole trip.

When she arrived in East Boston, no one was there to meet her. She searched the crowd of faces and waited, but no one came to greet her. She always told me this story and I can hear her now saying, "When I landed in East Boston, I didn't have a penny to my name." Even years later her voice sounded like a lost soul, desperate, scared, and nervous. I imagine that she wondered why she came. She said that was very scared and anxious to see her sister and brother. Eventually an official was able to get in touch with Margaret and Willie, and they came to get her. They had never received her letter; it was on the same boat she had been on from Ireland.

My maiden name is Brien, not O'Brien. When my dad came to this country, he dropped the "O" in the ocean. That was always a big joke with my dad; he just thought that was so funny. My parents met in Boston and married in 1937 at St. Mary's Chapel in the North End. They moved to Hillside Street in Mission Hill and when the projects opened up, they got an apartment there. That was the best thing to ever happen because there was lots of heat! The rent was a flat rate. My brother Billy

Jim Gurry, best man, my aunt Margaret Downey, my mother Beatrice, and my father William Brien

was born in 1939, followed by Peggy in 1941, Tommy in 1943, and me in 1946. There were three bedrooms—one for my parents, one for the boys, and one for Peggy and me. There were so many nice people in the Mission Hill Project; we were all struggling, living paycheck to paycheck. We were poor, but we kids didn't know it.

Aunt Margaret was a very special person in my life right from the day I was born. My mother took sick after my birth and Aunt Margaret took care of me until my mother recovered. Growing up, Thursday was my favorite day of the week because it was Aunt Margaret's day off. She was a domestic for Mrs. Steinert, of M. Steinert & Sons piano company. Aunt Margaret lived and worked at Mrs. Steinert's home at 401 Commonwealth Avenue, but she came to visit us often on her days off (Thursdays and every other Sunday). Aunt Margaret was very generous and always spent her money on us. We had delicious steak, rolls, and chocolate cake with buttercream frosting and walnuts. When it was time to have the cake, someone or maybe all of us scraped the frosting from the cake, but no one would own up to it. Every other Sunday, Aunt Margaret would come over and maybe take us downtown to a restaurant.

On the Sundays when Aunt Margaret worked, we kids visited her. We ran like crazy down Marlborough Street to see who could get to the back entrance first. Aunt Margaret would be waiting for us, and sometimes gave us each a Ritz cracker for a treat. The old elevator had black gates over the door and it was as slow as could be. We inched our way up from the first floor to the third floor, and Aunt Margaret would be very nervous, saying, "Be quiet, be quiet."

The kitchen had a dumbwaiter that went up to the third floor. It was used mostly for big parties held in the upstairs dining area.

We made do. Dad worked for Harvard as a janitor and caretaker, on Huntington and Longwood avenues. Mother did domestic work in the Back Bay with Aunt Margaret. Thursday was grocery day. My mother and I would meet my father at the First National grocery store with his paycheck. By the following Wednesday, Dad and I would be eating gravy sandwiches, leftover from roast beef made on Sunday.

One day I came home from school to find my mother reading a letter by the kitchen window. She had tears streaming down her face. I started crying, asking, "Ma, Ma, what's wrong?" She said, "This is a letter from home that says my mother has passed away." I was nine years old and I felt so bad for her; I couldn't imagine being without *my* mother. When I think about that now, her mother had probably passed at least a week or two before that letter arrived.

In 1957, my Aunt Margaret took me on a vacation to Ireland for five weeks. She wanted to take one of us kids and I don't remember anyone else volunteering to go. I was eleven years old, and so excited. All my aunts and uncles in Boston gave me spending money for the trip. *The Roxbury Citizen* newspaper even printed a little story with a picture. It read, "Roxbury girl Ann Brien boards a Pan-American clipper to Ireland with her aunt Margaret Downey for five weeks."

It was my first time on a plane. We took a taxi out to the farm, near Athlone in County Roscommon, central Ireland. The landscape was wide open with beautiful green valleys. Walls of stacked stones fenced in the sheep and cattle. Coming from Roxbury, all of this open country was a big change.

Mother and Aunt Margaret's second oldest brother, Uncle Dennis, lived on the farm, ran the farm, and never left the farm — it was his whole life. The farmhouse had two levels, a fireplace, and a thatched roof, but no indoor plumbing. You had to go out to the barn to do your business. At home my mother always said, "In this country you go out to eat and come in to go to the bathroom, but in Ireland you go out to go to the bathroom and come in to eat." I suddenly understood what that meant. The kitchen had a cast-iron stove and no refrigerator; Uncle Dennis used a cold box with ice. Milk came from the cows and eggs from the hens. People came around selling bread and bakery goods. We went into town, where Uncle Dennis and other farmers sold their livestock.

Everything on the farm was new to me. I had never ridden a horse or milked a cow. All the farm work was an education in itself. I was very happy and excited to be there, but after a few days I was sad and lonesome for my mother, father, and family. I just cried day after day. I pulled out the money my aunts and uncles in Boston had given me for the trip and said, "I can buy my ticket back home," but Aunt Margaret explained that it wasn't possible for us to go back early. After a week, I started adjusting to the farm.

There was a huge painted portrait of my mother in the stairwell; she was a beautiful young lady, with dark black hair and big brown eyes. Seeing it made me miss her, but it also made me happy in that she was with me.

We visited the one-room schoolhouse my mother had attended. It was a small, plain room. There weren't enough desks for everyone, so chairs were clustered together around each desk.

Uncle Dennis let me ride up front with him on the wagon on our trips to the bog. The horse was old and slow. When we got to the bog, Uncle Dennis dug out pieces of peat the size of bricks and I helped load it into the wagon. Stepping on the bog was like walking on a sponge, like cork.

I loved the horses, cows, and chickens. I helped milk the cows, and I rode the horses. The baby chicks were so cute, so fluffy. One day I was out playing and thought I would give the baby chicks a treat. I filled a big basin of water and put them in so they could go for a swim, then I left them and went on to play somewhere else. Later, Uncle Dennis told Aunt Margaret, "The little one there put the baby chicks in the basin, and I found them all dead." Aunt Margaret then explained to me that chickens can't swim and that the baby chicks didn't survive. I felt so bad. After that, I still played around the barn, but didn't give any "treats" to the animals.

After a few weeks on the farm, Aunt Margaret and I left for the big city of Dublin. I imagine that after what happened to the chickens, Uncle Dennis was happy to see me go. Dublin felt a lot like Boston, busy and exciting, like being home again. I met many cousins there and had a lot of fun. I had never seen a double-decker bus, and I couldn't get over it. I always rode on the second level; Aunt Margaret would shout up to tell me when it was time to get off the bus. She was very patient. When it was time to leave Ireland I could feel the tears coming; yes, I was crying again. It was so hard to leave all my relatives, but I was very happy to be home with my family.

I was not fortunate enough to know or meet any of my grandparents like other kids my age. I had Aunt Margaret and she did a good job spoiling me. Thank you, Aunt Margaret, for everything you did for my family and me.

THANK YOU,
MOTHER ATKINSON

Julia Martin

My life is complicated in some ways. Some memories are sad and some are happy, as I moved from one family to another. My parents, Joseph Fontes and Adeline Baptiste, were from the Cape Verde Islands. They settled in a small town midway to Cape Cod—Wareham—where I was born on July 2, 1929. My mom and dad had four living children; two passed away and I was the oldest.

I remember the Depression in 1935. Things were very bad. I stood in long lines with Mom to get surplus food. Thank God, Mom was an excellent cook. She never baked or cooked without an apron on, and was always singing and dancing. She also liked to sew and made all my dresses. The best events were going to the beach every day, and I also went to dances with Mom.

Dad was a fisherman and sold fish and clams to fish markets. Mom made bread and sold it to make money. Dad also worked for the WPA. He helped build the Sagamore Bridge on Cape Cod in 1935.

I remember standing out on our dirt road, waiting for him to come home with his lunch pail of leftover goodies. During this time mom and dad fought all the time. The Depression and World War II interfered with many lives. Mom and Dad separated. When Mom left, she took the youngest child with her. My two brothers and I remained with Dad. He tried very hard to raise us, but he was crippled after being hit by a car. It was difficult for him to work and take care of us.

The worst day of my life came when I was in the seventh grade. I was in class when someone removed my two brothers and me from our classrooms and took us to court. I never went back to school that day. The three of us became wards of the state. I cried all day, afraid and embarrassed. My best friends saw me being removed and my brothers were gone. I was taken to Boston alone, and waited all day at the state house to be placed in a foster home. They gave me a black cardboard suitcase and filled it with new clothes.

Later that day, I was taken to a foster home. I was so afraid because I was in a big city full of tall buildings, riding on a train high off the ground that I found out later was called the el. I thought we were going to fall and crash. I was with a stranger. I didn't know where I was going and what was going to happen to me.

We arrived at 234 West Canton Street in the Back Bay neighborhood of the city. I met a very tall, fair-skinned, stern-looking woman. She checked me all over, and checked my hair for lice. I told her, "I don't have lice. My dad kept me clean." She replied, "Well, I still have to check you out." Then she said, "My name is Mrs. Atkinson. The children call me Mother, but you decide what you want to call me. It's your decision."

When it was time for supper, all the children sat at the nicely set dining room table. We had napkins with napkin rings, linen tablecloths, and nice china. First grace had to be said, the table had to be blessed. I didn't recognize this white thing on my plate. I remarked my dad had never given me cream of wheat with gravy, peas, and pork chops for dinner. I didn't want to eat it.

The other children replied that I was about to eat grits. I had never heard of grits. They explained that it was like rice. In my culture, the Cape Verdean food that my mother made, rice and beans was called "jag," not grits. They all laughed. I got a history that night about different foods, different cultures, and how you must eat everything on your dish.

I cried myself to sleep because I missed my dad and my brothers and friends. I didn't know where they were. I felt unloved, that my family abandoned me. What about school? I wondered. When will I go? It was a lonely time. I was moved around a lot, but I was placed back with Mother Atkinson and I stayed there until I was old enough to be on my own.

Mother Atkinson was strict but pleasant. She took care of fifteen girls and one boy, who she had cared for since infancy. He slept on the same floor she did, not where the girls slept. We lived on four floors of a brick house that Mother owned. It was clean and comfortable. There was lots of love, laughter, and chores to be done. I was the smallest in height, not the youngest. Mother only allowed me to run errands, go shopping, and pay bills. She said I was too tiny to do chores. We went to church every Sunday and on Holy days. I attended private parochial schools, and I graduated from St. Joseph's Academy in Roxbury.

I was enrolled in a bugle-and-drum corps called Arch Bishop Cushing. As cadets, we won several competitions in Boston. We attended the Blessed Sacrament on Vernon Street in Roxbury. After school, Sister Eugenia was well-known. She was strict and stern and yet so little, but we all loved her. We attended dancing only at the convent on Vernon Street or on weekends at the Abraham Lincoln Settlement House in the South End. Curfew was at ten o'clock sharp, or Mother Atkinson would be standing on Columbus Avenue disguised in a man's hat and trench coat in some doorway watching for her girls.

As teenagers, we knew we had better be on our best behavior. Our boyfriends would not be visible. They respected Mother Atkinson. "No hanky-panky," she would say. She always knew who our boyfriends were. We went to see the big bands that came to the RKO, Paramount Theater, and Loews Orpheum, but we had to earn our money. We would ask neighbors if they needed their backyard cleaned, errands done, or front steps swept and washed. We got our money together and enjoyed the shows—Count Basie, Duke Ellington, Ella Fitzgerald, Frank Sinatra, Mankie Lane, and many more. We stopped to enjoy Nemo's frankfurters and White Tower hamburgers or fried chicken, or we went to the deli on the corner of Washington Street and Essex. Those were the good old days.

Everyone on West Canton Street wanted to see what the state kids were wearing on the first day of school. Mother would line us up and say, "Hold your head up high for you are somebody. Always remember that." We paraded out to school with our heads up high. I still do it today.

At eighteen years old, you were discharged from the state to be on your own, provided that you had a job. I worked several jobs, and then went into nursing at the Children's Hospital. I was dating a fine young man—handsome, tall, a perfect gentleman. We dated for three years; everyone thought we would get married. Things happened and we did not marry. We broke up. Meanwhile I met my old girlfriend from Onset, Massachusetts. We had been childhood friends before I was sent to the foster home. She was married and she invited me to dinner. Her name was Mary Pina. Her cousin Eugene came home from work, and she introduced me to him, but then he disappeared. I asked Mary, "Your cousin is quite handsome, but why did he leave so quickly? Is he bashful?" After dinner, we were sitting around and Eugene reappeared, this time showered and dressed in a smart tie, white shirt, looking so handsome. We spoke for a while and I left to go back to the Children's Hospital dorm to get ready for classes the next day.

Two weeks went by when I got a call from Mary. Her cousin wanted to know when I was coming back to visit. I replied that I was dating someone else and I didn't know when I could get back to visit. Every week I would get a phone call. My boyfriend and I had gone away for Labor Day weekend to visit his family in New York. As he was writing a postcard to one of our friends, I put two and two together and realized that while I was in school, something must have been going on between them. I went back to Mary's house to make a date with her cousin Gene. He was also Cape Verdean, and had grown up in a foster home. What a small world. Gene had an automobile and he offered to drive me to Onset to see my dad. I was so excited.

After all those years I got to see my dad, my friends, my hometown, and my brother David, who was living in a foster home in Buzzard's Bay. I was floating on air. After a few more dates, Gene took me to visit his mother who had raised him. They lived in Wareham. She said, "He really must care for you; he has never brought anyone home before."

After three months of dating, we eloped and got married — such a short romance. We expected our first baby and I was excited. I intended to go back to nursing, but my family increased every two years. Our marriage had good and bad times, up and downs, but we were "for better or worse until death do us part." After twenty-six years of marriage, he had a massive heart attack and passed away on April 1, 1972. We had five children — three boys and two girls.

I wasn't the only one of Mother Atkinson's children to have a happy life. Mother's children all grew up to be well-respected adults. They studied and had jobs as nurses, government workers, a chef's assistant, and an undercover detective. Mother's girls are all great parents as well. I still know many of them today. We still get together to talk about old times. Being a state kid (or what they call today a DSS kid) doesn't mean that the child is bad. I feel I turned out to be okay for a state kid. Thank you, Mother Atkinson.

BASEBALL,
AN AUTOGRAPH BOOK,
AUNT CLARA, EINSTEIN,
AND ME

Gloria Wright

Good afternoon baseball fans. Today, facing the cross-town rival Giants, the crowd's hoping to see Don Newcombe pitch his best game. It would be a real thrill to see him load up the bases and strike out the next three batters. Newk is an ex-navy man who spent two years in the Pacific theatre.

Growing up in the bucolic college town of Princeton, New Jersey, during the forties and fifties, radio was a constant companion, a link to big-city New York and the rest of the world. From early morning to late night, we tuned in to the swing sounds of Jimmy Dorsey, Lionel Hampton, and Cab Calloway; radio soap operas *Helen Trent* and *Our Gal Sunday;* and the news of the day. Stretching from afternoon into the early hours of the next morning, we reclined in the cool of my Aunt Clara's porch and listened to baseball—the Brooklyn Dodgers versus just about

anyone, but mostly I lived to hear them play against their archrivals, the New York Giants.

The voice of Red "The Ol' Redhead" Barber was synonymous with my team. I enjoyed hearing his detailed and folksy descriptions of the game. I still think of lying on the daybed listening to Red saying kind things about each player. He concentrated not only on their exploits on the field but also who they were as people.

My aunt Clara Banks lived on Springfield Road. She was a big woman—five foot eleven, large-framed with long arms and legs. She smoked and worked at the same time without ever dropping ashes from her Chesterfield cigarette. She was a dear friend, mother, and confidante to me. Of my five brothers and sisters, I was the one singled out to help her iron, cook, clean, sew, or anything else she needed. My mother's oldest living sister, she had named me at birth and that began our bond.

I always felt good about being her pet and learning how to do things the right way. She was a gourmet chef and taught me how to cook, and also taught me the crafts of knitting, crocheting, and embroidery. She always asked to hear about the books I read. In those days, I'd get a book and stay up all night reading. What sealed our relationship for all time was baseball. In the evenings after work, we would sit on her screened side porch, eat a meal of skillet-fried chicken, bread, and iced tea, and listen to the games over the small brown box. Though living in Jersey, our team was the Dodgers. Brooklyn had some of the most colorful and interesting players.

In 1947, Jackie Robinson broke through the color barrier and came to the Dodgers as the first African American ball player in the Major Leagues. Within a few years, there were several others who joined him on the team, including Roy Campanella, Don Newcombe, Joe Black, Jim Gilliam, and Sandy Amoros. They changed the game not only due to their race but also by their excellent play.

Since the dog days of August began, the Dodgers have been tearin' up the pea patch. We're in the top of the second, at home, the bases are F.O.B. Robbie takes a lead off first, having laid down a perfect bunt that lazily rolled up the third base line, moving Campy to third and Reese to second. Now, Mister Snyder steps to the plate, batting at .315; Big fella Hatten pitches it in there for strike one!

Princeton reminded me of Peyton Place. It was a small college town that ringed a main boulevard, Nassau Street. Princeton College took up one side of the avenue while stores, three banks, two theaters, and a preppy shop had the other side. There were three taxis

Gloria's autograph book

and one bus that traveled along Nassau, but everyone walked, biked, or drove to work — mostly walked. I was a great walker in those days and knew just about everyone there. The town had several millionaires, and my aunt worked for some of those wealthy families.

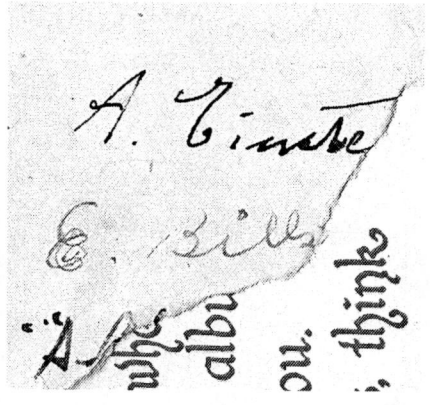

Partial Albert Einstein signature

The owners of Johnson & Johnson and playwright George Bernard Shaw lived there but, of all the well-known people, Princeton had one superstar: Dr. Albert Einstein, the most famous scientist of modern times. He came to Princeton in 1933 to accept a position at the Institute of Advanced Study. Folks often whispered about him, expressing an interest in meeting him. Daily on my way to Aunt Clara's, I would walk past his house on Mercer Street. To my teenage eyes he looked very strange. He wore a big blue knitted hat pulled down over his shockingly white hair. He'd have on one boot and one galosh, as he steadied a black pipe at the left side of his mouth. His coat didn't have buttons but was held together by a big safety pin. I wanted to stop and talk to him, but was definitely afraid because he looked like a hermit. After I told my aunt that I saw him frequently, she gave me an autograph book on my fifteenth birthday to get his signature. She'd never met Dr. Einstein but was curious.

The autograph book was made of green leather with a zipper around it, the word, "Autograph" inscribed in gold in its center. I thought about how to approach him every day as I passed his house. Finally, one day I walked up and waited. When he came out, I introduced myself and said in a little voice, "Dr. Einstein, may I have your autograph, please?" He looked at me with his deep dark eyes—the eyes were really frightening—then abruptly took my hand and walked me to his school. At the institute, he sat me down on a little bench and talked to me about his life. He lectured me about different mushrooms that grew under trees, spoke about a little boy that he tutored in math, and even shared details about his second wife and the first one whom he'd divorced. We talked about a lot of things then he eventually signed my book. After that, when I encountered him on his way to Edgerly Road, I was no longer afraid of him.

Shortly before, my Aunt Clara had received several prized autographs. New York and New Jersey were known to be hot and humid in the summer. If folks weren't at Ebbets Field cheering the Dodgers, at the Polo Grounds watching the Giants, or at Yankee Stadium in the Bronx, it seemed everyone left the city — even players — for a chance to go swimming at the beach. We would go to Bel Mar, Point Pleasant, or Atlantic City to hang on the Jersey shore. Beaches were good places to meet ball players and other athletes. My aunt got to know several Dodgers well, especially Roy Campanella. One day, he gave Aunt Clara a baseball with all the players' autographs on it. He was a very nice family man and had gathered the signatures for her as a surprise. It was signed by pitchers Joe Black, Sandy Koufax, and Don Newcombe; infielders Gil Hodges, Pee Wee Reese, and Jackie Robinson; outfielders Sandy Amoros, Carl Furillo, and Duke Snider; and of course catcher Campanella. That autograph ball became my aunt's prized possession. She kept it in a small white box on her mantel for all the family to see.

Back, back, back, back, back, back...heeee makes a one-handed catch against the bull pen! Oh, doctor!

When I think back on the early fifties and that old autograph book, I marvel at how many memories are contained in a simple stroke of a pen. Unzipping the worn book, I open to a page where my aunt wrote some words of encouragement to me. Dr. Einstein's signature is on the first page, a quarter of it having been torn away by rambunctious grandnieces and grandnephews. I peer at its strange swirls and recall his voice asking, "What would happen if you could catch up the beam of light frozen in time?"

The pastimes of radio, baseball, and Einstein that I shared with my aunt were like beams of light, and the autographs we garnered served to freeze our precious memories in time. We listened to Jackie Robinson withstand taunts and jeers for opening doors in baseball. In 1955, we finally saw him win the World Series at Ebbets Field, the first African American to do so. We sunned on the beach with Campanella, winner of three MVP awards, before an automobile accident cut his career short. I strolled arm-in-arm with Dr. Einstein during his latter years as a renowned but humble scientist at Princeton. In 1951, my aunt purchased a black-and-white television set to watch the games on, and gradually radio faded into the distance. I've kept the worn green autograph book to this day. Aunt Clara's baseball hung around for many years following her passing in 1962 and then disappeared. It's been rumored that a grandson may have sold it on eBay. Despite its loss, I've retained the memory of my favorite aunt who shared her many passions with me.

A PORTRAIT OF
NANA DOHERTY

Joan Flynn

The famous painting known as *Whistler's Mother* always reminds me of my grandmother, Hannah Josephine Kelleher Doherty. I remember first seeing the image as a young child of seven or eight. Like the woman in the painting, Nana Doherty dressed very plainly. She always wore an apron over a cotton housedress and black lace-up shoes with a low heel. She wore no makeup except for a little face powder on occasion. I can still picture her combing her hair and making a long grey braid down her back and over her shoulder. She then twisted the braid into a "pug" (a bun) and used bone hairpins to lock it in place. I never knew her age until she died. As a child, I always thought she was old.

I don't really remember deciding to live with Nana and Papa, but most of the time I did stay with them, from age six or seven on. I went back and forth. My parents' home had a toilet but no bath. We had to bathe in the kitchen sink and I didn't like that. I had an older brother and a younger brother, and whenever one of us had to

bathe, we kids would yell, "Don't come in the kitchen—I'm getting washed!" I might have started staying at Nana's because I slept on the couch at home, but at Nana's I could sleep in a bed. Aunt Frannie (Frances) lived with Nana and Papa during the war while her husband served in the navy. Aunt May (Mary) lived with them until she married. Sometimes there would be four of us crowded into the double bed, two at the head and two at the foot. On cold nights Nana would put coats on top of us to keep us warm.

When I was very little, I had rheumatic fever and was very sick. I remember going to see Dr. English for my heart murmur and he said, "If you gain half a pound, we'll have a prize for you when you come back!" When I had one of my frequent earaches, Nana would heat some oil and drop it into my ear.

Nana Doherty was born in Boston in 1881 and lived her entire eighty-nine-year life here. As far as I know, Nana did not have much of life's pleasure, or any formal education. I remember five different apartments around Roxbury and Jamaica Plain where Nana and Papa lived during my childhood. Before that, they lived in the Leaky Roof tenements on Downing Street in Roxbury. When Papa came home tipsy, he would shuffle his feet as if dancing and say he was "loose as ashes." At one time Nana worked cleaning rooms at the Statler Hotel in the South End. In later years, my aunts had to hide her shoes and hat to keep her from going back to the Statler to ask for work.

Aunt May and Aunt Frannie worked at Armour Meat Packing on Columbus Avenue. They liked to take me shopping downtown on Saturdays to Jordan's and Filene's for shoes and clothes. I loved

Shirley Temple and Aunt May bought me a Shirley Temple coat, dress, and doll. They went to millinery stores and had special hats made for them. It was fun to watch Aunt Fran get all dressed up to go dancing every week. I watched as she put on her makeup and jewelry. Fran was a champion jitterbug dancer and one time she won a silver cup.

Nana Doherty

The family came together every Saturday at Nana's for her baked beans, made in her bean pot with melted brown sugar, salt pork, and onion. Uncle Owen spread the fat from the salt pork on toast and ate it. Aunt Frannie and Aunt May, Uncle Johnny and Uncle Owen, my parents, and various cousins crowded into the apartment. On Sundays, Nana made boiled dinner — pork shoulder, boiled beets and vinegar, potatoes, cabbage, turnips, and onion. During the week, she turned those leftovers into bubble and squeak — leftover vegetables stirred together in a frying pan. It was delicious. There were no big supermarkets then, and I went to the corner store to buy groceries for Nana. She had me put the cost on her tab, and the tab was always running.

Nana's big black stove was always hot and served as the main source of heat for the apartment. It had beautiful chrome edging, and Nana cleaned and polished the stove frequently with black iron-stove polish. In the winter, we would open the oven door and warm our feet. We also hung our wet socks and mittens on the oven door to dry. It burned coal, wood, or newspapers, and a large pipe attached it to the chimney. Coal was expensive and we rarely had it. Sometimes, Nana would walk along the Roxbury train tracks to gather coke that had fallen out of the engines. At home, we twisted newspaper into knots so they burned longer. The stovetop had four heavy round burner covers, and we used a cover lifter that had a coiled handle and a curved iron prong to gain entry to the fire portion. The stove had a back wall with a shelf where the salt and pepper was kept. There was also an oven area for baking that Nana used to cook beans. In a small tin frying pan, she melted brown sugar for the molasses on the beans. She boiled soiled handkerchiefs in a big pot on the stovetop; there were no Kleenex tissues then.

It seemed like Nana was always taking care of everyone in the family: washing clothes for Frannie, May, or Papa on the old scrub board; ironing shirts and pants; and cleaning the house. She faithfully scrubbed the front stairs every week. Nana was very religious and went to Mass every day. When I was at her house, I went to Mass with her. She was very strict in a quiet way. I liked to whistle a lot as a girl; I still do. Nana told me many times to stop, saying, "When a girl whistles, the Blessed Virgin Mary cries." On summer evenings, I had to be in the house by the ninth chime of the Mission Church bells. In the winter, I had to be home by the seventh chime.

I went back and forth between my parents' home and Nana's from elementary until high school. When I started working at Woolworth's five-and-dime store at age fourteen, my father said, "I want her home," but really he just wanted the money I was earning. My father was ill and unable to work; my parents needed the money to survive. When I graduated from high school, I worked in the office at Armour's on Columbus Avenue with my aunts.

My Nana was a very kind and loving person who always worked at trying to please everyone. She died peacefully in her home in West Roxbury in 1970 at age eighty-nine.

Modern Ali Babas

CAMMENARE DIRETTA
(WALK A STRAIGHT LINE)

Alice Palumbo

I was born in 1923 in Readville, Massachusetts, a section of Hyde Park. My parents were first-generation Italian immigrants. I was the sixth girl in a family of eleven — six girls and five boys. My mother was widowed at age forty-eight and left to raise her eleven children alone.

She was lucky, though. She had land on which to grow fruits and vegetables in Hyde Park. All of us did our share. The boys took care of the gardens and the girls helped with making preserves, cooking, and cleaning. During harvest time, we preserved tomatoes, vinegar, roasted peppers, grape jelly, peaches, and cherries. The smell of the preserves permeated the house and garden — it was so delicate. I especially liked when Mom made piccalilli with the small, unripe tomatoes. I loved the pepper relish she made. I have never found that taste in store-bought relish.

I learned a lot from my humble beginnings. We always ate well. Mom made homemade bread, cakes, and good old-fashioned biscotti. When the apples fell after a windy day, we gathered them up. Mom peeled and sliced them very thin. With a beautiful smile on her face, she'd make a pinwheel with the apples and put them on top of a cake, sprinkle it with sugar, and we'd have it after our big Sunday dinner.

Every Sunday was an open house at the Imbaro's. Mom always wanted our friends to come over so she could keep an eye on us. We made our own entertainment. We gathered around the pianola. My brother Chickie never took a lesson but could play anything. Josie also played and sang soprano, and we all took turns pumping the pianola. My youngest brother Guido was a comedian and impersonator.

My sisters were very smart; they knitted, crocheted, and made intricate lace called tatting. I tried so hard, but all I made were knots and more knots. My sisters were very talented in the domestic arts, but by the time I came along, no one had the patience to teach me. I went to Girls' Trade School in the Fenway where I learned dressmaking and interior decorating, but I didn't like it. When I graduated in 1941, there was little work because of the war. I worked at home for a while as a seamstress, but no one was buying men's clothing. I felt stupid and insignificant. The war was getting closer and I felt like I needed to do something.

One day my friend Mary asked me to go downtown with her so she could join the Women's Army Corps (WACs). She didn't know how to get to the Saltonstall Building, so I went along to keep her company. When we entered the elevator, I saw a poster of a female marine. It was stunning and I fell in love with the uniform. When the elevator stopped at the army recruiting floor, Mary got off. I said, "I'm going up to the fourth floor. I'm going to join the marines." I enlisted in the U.S. Women's Reserve or the WR. I was called in for a physical in December 1944. I always say that when they saw me coming, the war ended.

When I received my orders to report for duty in the Women's Reserve, I had to go to South Station to get the train to Camp Lejeune, North Carolina. It was so cold. I can still remember my teeth chattering. My coat was thin, and I had a cheap cardboard suitcase and a large manila envelope under my arm. Before I left home, Mom said, "Remember, wherever you go, look people straight in the eye and always tell the truth. No matter where you go, you might meet people who will know you or someone in the family." I always felt her eyes on me; I think it was her prayers that followed me around.

The first thing I remember about Camp Lejeune was meeting a stern, young female marine in a beautiful forest green uniform. Her dress hat had a large Marine Corps emblem in the center with a red cord knotted beneath. It was the most beautiful uniform I had ever seen. The three red chevrons on her sleeves meant that she was a sergeant. Her posture was squared off, a term used in the Corps that meant perfect. She was a little bit of a person with a big voice. She yelled, "Attention!" We lined up. Then she yelled, "Look at the person to your left! Look at the person to your right! One of you might not make it through boot camp!" "Oh," I thought, "I've got to make it!"

We marched a lot and sang military songs as we marched. We cleaned and scrubbed. We got a lot of inoculations and then scrubbed some more to relieve the pain of the shots. There were always dust inspections in the barracks, and we learned how to swab the decks. Personal hygiene was a big issue. We ran through the showers every day, with only minutes to wash and dress. It was very important that our shoes were never very far away from us. If there was an emergency, we had to drop everything, run and make sure we had our shoes—if not on our feet, then under our left arm. That was drilled into me. If we were called to battle, our shoes protected us in all kinds of emergencies. Even today, sixty years later, I always know where my shoes are.

Sloshing through the swamps of North Carolina was frightening, and riding in those huge trucks made my stomach queasy. We had to go out on an LCP (Landing Craft, Personnel) and the boat ride was rough. When the boat hit the shore with a swift bang, the portside panel flew down and we had to run like hell! I thought I was the only one who got seasick. When I looked around, it seemed as if the whole squadron was bent over with the heaves. I laugh now, but it wasn't so funny then. The worst dry heaves I ever had was when we had to go through the teargas tents. I thought my eyes would come out of my head. All I could think was, "Am I going to make it?" I looked around and saw many of the other "boots" coughing and choking with tears running down their cheeks.

We all had to do guard duty. My night on River Road was scary. The campus was on one side of the street and the river and the woods were on the other. I had to walk my post with a flashlight and a billy club. It was a cold night, and I was bundled up with a heavy trench coat and scarf. Suddenly I heard footsteps coming towards me. I yelled out, "Who goes there?" No response. At the end of the post was a young Dutch male marine. It's a good thing I didn't have a rifle or I might have blown him away!

Being down south during the days of segregation is still vivid in my memory. During my first eight-hour pass, I took a bus to Raleigh, North Carolina. Being from Boston, where we could sit anywhere, I didn't know about any restrictions on buses. I walked up to the back. I felt all eyes were on me. I thought it was because of my beautiful uniform, all shiny and new against my white complexion and big smile. I sat back comfortably. When I got off the bus, I waited for it to pass so I could cross the street. The door was still open. The bus driver bent over, called me a "damn Yankee" and spit out the door at me. How did he know I was a Yankee, I wondered? When I got back to the barracks and told my friends what had happened, I found out the meaning of the word segregation.

I left the marines in 1946. My brother Frank was wounded in the war and suffered two years in and out of intensive care at the VA Hospital. He died in 1947. The street we grew up on was renamed Imbaro Road after my dear brother. My mother's heart was broken, but she never stopped loving America. She was so proud the day she got her citizenship. Mom couldn't read or write, but she learned all the names of the politicians and joined many civic organizations.

My husband was on the *St. Paul* during Japan's surrender ceremony at the end of the war. We were married in 1949 and he was called back for the Korean War. Our son was born nine months later.

My husband didn't get to see our firstborn until his son was three months old. When he came home from the Korean War, he never wanted to leave the house. We never had a babysitter; one of us had to be home unless there was an emergency. We had a blessed marriage. Two years later we had a beautiful daughter.

My husband died at the age of fifty-four. He might have been contaminated by nuclear fallout when he was on the ship. After he was discharged, he suffered from breathing problems and died from interstitial lung disease. He got sick on Mother's Day and died on Father's Day. He is always in my heart. I thank God for the beautiful, peaceful life he gave us. When he died, I got no financial assistance or veteran's benefits. I babysat and did alterations on women's clothing. I was inspired by Mom's example. Both my children paid for their college educations and have master's degrees. I am thankful that they were able to get the education I only dreamed about.

Like my mother, I am very active in my community. I can look people straight in the eye when I talk to them. I've always taken her advice to heart: *cammenare diretta,* "walk a straight line."

THE TRIPS OF MY LIFE

LOS VIAJES DE MI VIDA

Héctor Rivera

Translated by Jennifer De Leon

Traducido por Jennifer De Leon

189

JAMAICA PLAIN

In Spanish, we have many sayings. In the Latino culture, we have many traditions. Although these sayings are not attached to specific dates in history, they are universal. They are unlike many of the traditions that are marked on the calendar of life. We do not always know where they come from or, most importantly, who created them or why they are recalled. Many sayings have dual meanings. For example, one saying goes, "If you open it, shut it; if you drop it, pick it up; if they ask for bread, feed them; if they cry, comfort them, love them." Indeed, there are many meanings. Any single saying can educate you profoundly and show you a new facet of life in addition to other life lessons.

I grew up with the privilege and the wisdom that sayings—like traditions and proverbs—are very important. Words are vital. Often, we do not have other ways or means to pass on our traditions. In this way, the words and the stories can be like cameras of the soul. For me, trips have had a great influence, not only in my life, but also in the lives of my parents and my children. There is a saying that goes, "To travel is to live." I agree! I would add, "To travel is to live is to write!"

I.

Nothing was planned for this particular trip. Nothing was known. I spent my childhood years attending primary school. Daily life continued as usual. My dear mother would always tell me, "Study hard, because one day God will reward you with a big prize." I would ask her, "Like the lottery?" and she would laugh. She was always singing, "Study and persevere." I attended my small sixth-grade graduation ceremony and took many pictures. One day a letter arrived from New York where my Aunt Carmen lived. As a gift for my achievements in school, she had sent a plane ticket from Puerto Rico to New York with my name on it. This was how I came to visit the United States for the first time. The trip came as a result of my studies. This was a big lottery prize.

II.

I had come to Boston for a two-week holiday vacation. It was a beautiful, hot summer day in July 1964. What courted me was not the pretty, dark-skinned female on the street corner or the dazzling blonde, blue-eyed lady that chatted with her friend in the small park. It was the beautiful and cultural city of Boston. It was not my first experience in America. I had seen the green plains of the majestic countryside of Kentucky when I was in the United States Army. I had seen the blue water of the pretty beaches of Miami, and the immense skyscrapers of the grand New York City. Even though I had visited Boston other times, this time I fell in love with a new charm, a city so full and so rich with culture, beauty, history, and tradition that it was a dream of mine to stay, and to one day make this dream a reality. I still live here.

III.

In history books, I read old stories of travelers visiting new places as if they were Ali Baba. The great explorers were dreams for me until the day I met Boston. This trip made me dream more, and adopt the ongoing acts of knowing, living, seeing, and becoming one of Boston's most beloved foster children. Here I am today, still knowing, and living, another son of this beautiful place that is called Boston.

IV.

In his youth, my father, Don Pepe, had been a gravedigger. It was his only experience. When his son sent him a one-way plane ticket to move to Boston, he reached a golden, lifelong dream. Upon his arrival in Boston — seeing the skyscrapers and broad boulevards, the abundant traffic, and crowds of people walking attentively — he finally got to know and experience the fruits of his labor.

En Español, tenemos muchos dichos y en la cultura Latina tenemos muchas tradiciones. Aunque los dichos no tienen fechas, son universales. Al contrario, muchas de las tradiciones si tienen sus fechas porque marcan en el calendario de la vida, donde surgen, de donde vienen y lo mas importante, quienes las crearon y el porque se recuerdan. Muchos de los dichos tienen doble sentido. Por ejemplo: "Si tu los abres, ciérralos; si los dejas caer, recógelos; si te piden pan, aliméntalos; si te lloran, quiéralos, ámalos." Verdaderamente, hay muchos significados. Los dichos nos educan mas profundamente y nos enseñan otra nueva fase de la vida a través de las otras enseñanzas.

Yo crecí con el privilegio de la sabiduría que los dichos, como tradiciones, como proverbios, son *muy* importantes. Las palabras son vitales. A veces no tenemos otros tipos, o otras maneras de entregar nuestras tradiciones. De esta manera, las palabras y los cuentos pueden ser como cámaras del alma. Para mí, viajar ha sido una influencia grande, no solamente en mi vida, sino tambien en la vida de mis padres y mis hijos. Hay un dicho que dice así: Viajar es vivir. ¡Estoy de acuerdo! Yo añadiría: ¡Vivir es escribir!

I.

Nada estaba planificado de este viaje. Nada se sabía. Pasé mi niñez en la escuela primaria y la vida cotidiana continuaba como de costumbre. Solamente mi madre adorada me decía, "Estudia fuerte, porque algún día, Dios te recompensará con el premio grande." Siempre me cantaba, "Estudia y persevera." Así llegó mi graduación del sexto grado y después de las ceremonias saqué muchas fotos. Un día llegó una carta de Nueva York de mi tía Carmen. Ella había mandado un pasaje a mi nombre como un regalo a mi esfuerzo. Así fue como llegué a Nueva York por primera vez como un regalo de estudios. El premio fue mas grande que la lotería.

II.

Llegué a Boston para unas vacaciones breves de dos semanas en un bonito y caliente día de verano. Era julio de 1964. No me enamoré de la linda morena parada en la esquina, ni de la rubia deslumbrante de ojos azules que conversaba con su amiga en el pequeño parque, sino de la ciudad bella y culta de Boston. No fue mi primera experiencia de ver América. Yo había visto las llanuras verdes y el campo majestuoso de Kentucky cuando estaba en el ejército de los Estados Unido. Había visto las aguas azules de las playas lindas de Miami, y los rascacielos inmensos de la majestuosa ciudad de Nueva York. Aunque había visitado a Boston antes, esta vez me enamoré de su encanto nuevo, de una ciudad llena de la cultura, la historia, la belleza y la tradición. Quedarme aquí en Boston era mi sueño y yo lo realicé porque volví y todavía aquí vivo.

III.

Yo había leído en los viejos libros de historia los viejos cuentos de aquellos viajeros caminantes marineros como si fueran los cuentos de Ali Baba. Pero estos cuentos de los grandes exploradores fueron nada más que sueños hasta que conociera a Boston. Aquel viaje a Boston despertó mi sueño, y me quedé con la sola idea de conocerla, vivirla, y convertirme en uno de sus más queridos hijos adoptivos. Y aquí estoy como en el principio, todavía conociéndola, viviéndola, convertido en otro hijo más de esta bella leyenda que se llama: Boston.

IV.

En su juventud, mi padre, Don Pepe, era sepulturero. Era su única experiencia. Después de eso, no sabía hacer más nada. Por eso, cuando su hijo le mandó el pasaje para trasladarse para Boston, se cumplió un sueño dorado de su vida. Al llegar a Boston y ver los rascacielos, las avenidas grandes, el tráfico abundante, y el gentío de la gentes caminando apresuradamente, llegó a ver el fruto de su trabajo.

LOCKED IN A CEMETERY

Robert F. Hannan

On a late October afternoon, there's not much time before the sun starts to sink and darkness settles in. The air begins to get a bit nippy. Still, that wasn't of great concern as I cruised at a moderate speed on the roadway. Trees spaced in the preserve on either side of the road wore their fall finery of fashionable foliage. In the quiet gathering of dusk, I was really in no great hurry. I wasn't concerned by the absence of another vehicle. In fact, I quite expected to be alone — alone except for the two four-footed companions in the back seat. My thoughts wandered and focused on nothing more vital than, "I wonder what's for supper?"

We crested a small bluff (really just a rise) and the view became a little better and broader as the trees got sparser. The turn-off exit was ahead and then it was a couple of miles home. Overhead, the autumn sky was still clear but the slight suggestion of shadows was evident. "Ah, here's the clearing and ahead the gateway." I thought.

Then there was a sudden pall. The sweet, placid scene turned sour. Those friendly beckoning gates loomed as something else,

something hostile. Indeed they'd turned into a formidable barrier right then and there, set back in the semi-circular driveway off Walk Hill Street near the Mattapan section of Dorchester. Alas, as I nosed up to the exit, a harsh reality set in: I was locked inside Mount Hope Cemetery for the night! How could this be happening to me? How dare the cemetery people just go home and leave me abandoned to the dark terrors of the night?

In a semi-panic, I nosed my vehicle up to the gate. My focus was how do we (including the dogs and the car) get free of this dilemma as inconspicuously as possible? Really, this was no time to study what I presumed must be an intricate grillwork pattern of the ancient gates or the masonry architecture of the grand approach to this active city cemetery. For all I knew, those majestic gates might be thirty, even forty feet soaring skyward, appropriate guardians of those who slept within.

Yes, I did rue with a passing thought of embarrassment that I had neglected the sign aside the gateway. This notice proclaimed that Mount Hope's winter schedule calls for a five o'clock closing, and the time now was quite after five.

It was, for sure, time for exploratory action. Getting out on the pavement seemed the first thing to do. Exploring along the fence to the right toward the main office was a logical beginning. I found a space at a far corner of the building, an opening one could squeeze through, that was shielded by a fir tree probably eight feet tall. It provided an exit fit for man or dog. Knowing a route to freedom was at least helpful—but not for the automobile sitting inside the main gateway.

If it became absolutely necessary, I could make my way home on foot for a couple of miles. Of course with a black Labrador retriever and a white-with-black-and-brown-spots Jack Russell terrier trudging alongside, it would be a challenge. Such a venture in the gathering darkness on turning, twisting Harvard Street, known as the "cemetery road," could be a hazardous trek amidst constant traffic. (Even writing this late at night makes me feel for the seat belt.) In the time before I had a cell phone there was no way to communicate my plight to the outside world.

Things had seemed much brighter earlier in the day when I stopped at the cemetery office to get instruction on the burial site of three prominent people in the old town of Hyde Park, before it had become part of Boston. I was seeking burial plots way back in the spacious cemetery where abolitionist Theodore Weld, who died in 1895, was buried. The hunt was also for the two Grimke sisters, two southern belles who renounced their ancestral plantation heritage to become ardent, celebrated abolitionists as well as suffragettes. Angeline Grimke Weld had predeceased her husband by sixteen years in 1879. Her sister Sarah Grimke had gone to Mount Hope almost six years earlier in 1873.

Before and during the Civil War, the three were known in the Union area as ardent speakers and writers against the practice of slavery. Later they concentrated on the cause of women's suffrage, among other liberal pursuits. In March 1870, they marched as part of a group on the Hyde Park town election. Despite jeers, they made history when women voted in a school committee election for the first time in America, never mind that their ballots were cast in a separate tally box.

My cemetery vigil was supposed to be a quick errand. I thought it would be appreciated if I got a picture of the graves for Bill Drayton, a "veddy" British gentleman (accent to match) of St. John's Road, Christchurch, U.K., who was a descendent of the Grimkes. His research had led him to my wife, Nancy, who had been the long-time president of the Hyde Park Historical Society before her passing in February 2008.

My quest to find and snap a Polaroid picture just wasn't to be. I trudged several times back and forth on what I figured to be Evergreen Walk, charted as between and paralleling two roadways. Even with a small map provided, locating the graves was difficult because roadways of the cemetery, which had been established in 1851, have few name signs in the back area.

While I dislike quitting before a task is complete, common sense convinced me that trudging the same course back and forth, seeing the same headstones toppled to the ground, wasn't a productive pursuit. Better to try another day, I reasoned. So, after rounding up the dogs from their own explorations, I reluctantly headed out.

Now for the rest of the story.

Emerging on foot outside the cemetery, I spotted a two-tone blue vehicle. It was a Boston police car parked near the cemetery office building. The two officers in the car were surprised and maybe also bemused at my plight, then one of them remembered a primitive access point way over on the edge of the cemetery down Curley Street to Canterbury Street running behind the American Legion Highway shopping plaza. The officers said they'd check it out. Off they went on their mission. In perhaps a quarter hour or so, they were back with disappointing news. That remote gateway was also padlocked!

The patrolmen radioed or phoned their E-18 base in Cleary Square to appraise the situation. They emerged from their vehicle to report help was on the way. In another twenty minutes, maybe twenty-five, as the sun sank lower in the autumn sky, help arrived in the form of a single fire engine dispatched from the Blue Hill Avenue station in Mattapan. As the reddish vehicle turned in, I believe it emitted a low-growl siren sound, probably attesting the low priority of the firefighters' rescue assignment.

Out jumped a Jake with a huge pair of shears. I wondered if cutting a link or two in the wrap-around chain would be sufficient. The firefighter, trained for action, cut to the chase. He severed the padlock at the heart of the problem. Voilà! The gates, now all of ten feet or so in height, were swung free and open.

Expressing thanks but still quite embarrassed, I walked through to the car with its waiting, barking canine occupants. I didn't dare turn and witness the amused smiles of the combined fire and police forces at the scene.

I made a mental note to write to the mayor and offer to reimburse for the cost of the padlock — even though as a taxpayer I must have contributed to its purchase over the years. (Incidentally, I never did get a bill from His Honor.)

As I departed, turned right on Walk Hill Street and again right on Harvard Street, the "cemetery road," another thought occurred. In only a few days a significant occasion was due.

With a vision of Charlie Brown, Lucy, and the Great Pumpkin, I wondered what it would have been like if I had been locked in a cemetery on Halloween night!

EVERY TIME I RIDE THE GREYHOUND BUS, MY LIFE CHANGES

CADA VEZ QUE MONTO EL AUTOBÚS DE GREYHOUND, MI VIDA CAMBIA

Steve Quintana

Translated by Jennifer De Leon

Traducido por Jennifer De Leon

First Departure:
Ferry from Havana, Cuba, to Miami, Florida

February 24, 1957

Fidel Castro was still in "the mountains," as we say, when my parents decided the situation in Havana was dangerous enough for us to move. An uncle in Brooklyn helped us secure visas to the United States. My father knew a little English, but he was nowhere near fluent. At midnight on the evening of February 24, 1957, my parents and I left our homeland. I said goodbye to Cuba when I was just sixteen years old. By many standards I was grown, already six feet two inches tall. Looking back, I see I was just a boy inside a man's body.

The ferry ride from Cuba to Florida took about five or six hours. It was just the three of us — my mother Isabel, my father Esteban, and me. I was an only child. I did not know what to expect in America. The plan was to stay together as a family, work hard, and make a good life. Although I was born with the dream of becoming an artist, I was unsure whether I would be able to accomplish this goal in a new country. During my childhood in Cuba, my mother supported my hobby. She was always encouraging. Still, I was uncertain what the future would bring.

We arrived in Key West first before going to Miami to exchange official documents. The customs officials led us into a small room where we had to show our papers, including our visas and x-rays of

JAMAICA PLAIN

our lungs to show that we did not carry diseases such as tuberculosis. The embassy in Havana had taken care of all of that for us. My first meal in America was a plate of bland chicken and salad. It was not like Miami today where you can get many ethnic meals, but there was no time to complain. We had to meet our relatives in New York.

Greyhound Bus #1: One-way: Miami to New York City

February 25, 1957

During one of the stops the bus made, my dad thought there was time to buy a soda. We did not know it was an unofficial stop. In Cuba, the bus does not leave you. Here, the bus left my father. My mother and I were sleeping. When we realized what happened, my mother and I told the driver to return. He recommended that we get off at the next stop. Coincidentally, racial segregation was at its peak in the south. When we got off at the next bus stop and sat in the lounge, we did not realize we were sitting in the section for whites. A man told us to get out of there and to go to the section for the blacks. My mother did not understand that this place was reserved for white people and was forbidden to blacks. We were confused and angry.

We had to wait an hour for the next bus to come, the one that carried my dad. This was the first major experience in my first twenty-four hours in the United States. We stayed together for the rest of the journey. When we finally arrived in New York City, my mother's brother was waiting for us.

My uncle, Daniel Romero, was already a U.S. citizen living in New York. He welcomed us with coats and hot Creole food: rice and beans, fried plantains, and meat — real food. His family was happy to see us, especially because we arrived late.

My father began work as a dishwasher and my mother worked at a factory as a dressmaker, which had been her profession in Cuba. I also worked at a factory, assembling automobile parts. The year Fidel Castro took his position in Cuba, I began taking English classes at night in New York. Many of us worked at factories or stores during the day and studied at night. I also learned English little by little by watching movies. The problem today is that there are actually too many opportunities for people to speak Spanish. The need to learn English is not so urgent anymore. In the meantime, I tried to pursue my art whenever I could. An elderly Peruvian professor mentored me for a short time, but the arts scene slowed down in general, even music. Many older Dominican and Cuban artists began to die and with them, unfortunately, went much of their music. Today, I see that old men can't dance to modern music, and young men can't dance to old songs.

Music and Art

In the sixties and seventies, music played a major role in my life. I listened to Beny Moré, Sonora Matancera, Celia Cruz, Trio Matamoros, and Miguelito Valdez, Pérez Prado *(El Rey del Mambo)*, Tito Puente *(El Rey)*, Bobby Capó, Tito Rodriguez, Rafael Cortijo, and others. I combined my passion for art with my love for music, and I began to design record covers using watercolors and sometimes oil paints. I also worked on promotion for various musical performances and events and sometimes filled in for the DJ. I even got to do promotion for Don King at one point. During this time, salsa dancing became very popular. It originated in New York City. Even today, people can read about it, but they'll never truly know it, what it was to live it. In the Bronx, Queens, and Harlem, after-hours shows started at midnight and went until six in the morning. Men spun women on the dance floors, embracing different aspects of the old and the new traditions. There was a special rhythm to that time, much like the music. It was a fusion of many cultures, a *mex-cla*. There was harmony.

I developed my business as an artist and designer by offering to draw posters and advertisements for local Hispanic businesses, for example, beauty salons or even Goya. I created flyers, menus, even catalogs and magazines. Soon I had people working for me. I produced a magazine for the Santeria religion and people were glad, but they were also surprised and scared. They said, "You can't do that!" At the time, Santeria was still a private religion. Bit by bit, I became more involved in Santeria. Although I was aware of the religion in Cuba, I only began to fully understand it in New York. On December 25, 1982, I was initiated in a temple in East Elmhurst, Queens, as a *santero,* a spiritual priest.

Greyhound Bus #2: Roundtrip, New York City to New Jersey

1982

I met many people as I became more involved in Santeria and attended ceremonies and festivals. I first met my friend Olga at the Festival Patronas de Cuba in New Jersey. She lived in Boston. I began making weekend trips to Boston and staying at the Casa de Hospitalidad, a home she organized for many recent arrivals. Slowly I realized that there was a need for a Santeria congregation in Boston. There were no *botanicas* or places to practice the religion during this time. It was still secretive because people were afraid. Some people have confused Santeria with voodoo, witchcraft, and evil worship because we sometimes sacrifice animals in ceremonies. Chickens might be sacrificed to mark significant moments in life such as births, weddings, deaths, or initiations into the religion. I felt that there was a need for me in communities where people were afraid to practice something meaningful to them.

I believe it is important to keep tradition alive. After slaves were brought to Cuba from West Africa centuries ago, they combined the Yoruba African faith with Catholicism. A *santero* is a priest, but also a therapist, healer, mentor, and friend. As a *santero,* I help people who need to ward off curses or bad luck, or I suggest herbal remedies for life's everyday problems. Some people turn to chicken soup or aspirin to solve their problems. For us, an herbal tea or a brief ceremony could achieve the same remedy.

Greyhound Bus #3: One-way, New York to Boston

1987

After several years making a life in New York, I decided to move permanently to Boston. Even today, many people ask me, "Steve, why did you move to a new city when you had so many friends and family and strong business partnerships in New York?" I tell them that I was charmed by Boston's character and religious history. I decided to stay and build my own Santeria congregation, but only after I prayed and asked the saints if this was a good idea. I also wanted to help bring the religion out of its closet. I thought it was important to dispel myths and negative attitudes that people had about the religion.

In September 2005 I opened a *botanica* in Jamaica Plain called La Casa de Naturaleza. Now the store is located in Brighton. It is the Walgreens of the barrio. I help manage the store and continue my work as an ordained Obatala Priest of the Yoruba Religion. My cell phone rings all the time. Sometimes it is a young woman who is having trouble with a boyfriend. Other times it is a married couple having trouble conceiving a child, or someone who is experiencing *mal de ojo* or "evil eye." Financial troubles are common, too. Today, my mailing list has over two thousand names. Many people come to me before they go to a doctor. They visit my *botanica* before they go to the pharmacy. People come from many different places: Cuba, Puerto Rico, Brazil, Cape Verde, or Cambridge. They hear about me mostly by word-of-mouth. House of Obatala is the temple I keep inside my home off of Dorchester Avenue. There is a waiting room on the first floor, a shrine on the second floor, and a ceremonial room in the basement.

I also became a guest lecturer for an herbal tour of Boston with Boston University's School of Medicine Boston Healing Landscape Project. This project looks at cultural and religious beliefs of new immigrants. I think the medical students see me as an activist and a healer, but mostly I just want to help people. What many people do not realize is that often immigrants face language barriers, fear of cultural misunderstanding, or do not understand the healthcare system in the United States. Some do not have social security numbers. I do not think one way is better than the other. I want to be a bridge between immigrants and conventional doctors.

The only bus I take nowadays is the number 39 in Boston. Sometimes people ask if I would like to return to Cuba. Maybe one day I will return to my homeland, but only when the Communist regime is gone! For now, my home is the House of Obatala. Of the many lessons I have learned in life, the most valuable ones are to love freedom and to respect America. I have been able to accomplish so much here and to serve many people.

Primera Salida:
Ferry desde La Habana, Cuba a Key West, Florida

24 de Febrero del 1957

Me despidé de Cuba cuando tenía sólo dieciséis años de edad. Decíamos que Fidel Castro todavía estaba "en la montaña" cuando mis padres tomaron la decisión de mudarnos. La situación en Habana era demasiado peligrosa. Un tío que vivió en Brooklyn nos ayudó a conseguir las visas para ir a vivir en los Estados Unidos. Mi papá sabía hablar un poco del inglés, pero no para defenderse. Aun así dejamos nuestra patria al medianoche en el 24 de Febrero del 1957. Como yo media 188 cm de altura ya me parecía un adulto. Pero ahora me doy cuenta de que era apenas un niño en cuerpo de hombre.

El viaje en el tranbordador de Cuba a Florida tardaba cinco o seis horas. Éramos tres: mi mamá Isabel, mi papá Estebán, y yo. Yo era su único hijo. No sabíamos mucho de los Estados Unidos. Nuestro plan fue irnos como familia, trabajar duro, y seguir adelante. Aunque nací con el sueño de llegar a ser artista, dudaba en esa época si pudiera alcanzar aquella meta en mi país adoptivo. Durante mi niñez en Cuba, mi mamá siempre me apoyaba en el arte. Pero aún no sabía que me trajera el futuro.

Llegamos primero a Key West y de allí nos fuimos a Miami para entregar los documentos y pasar por las oficinas de inmigración. Los oficiales nos llevaron a un cuartito donde tuvimos que mostrar nuestros papeles, incluso los visas y también radiografías de los pulmones para comprobar que no llevábamos enfermedades como tuberculosis. Afortunadamente la embajada en Habana nos había arreglado todo esto. La primera comida que me dieron en Estados Unidos era un plato de pollo blando y una ensalada. En esos días no se encontraba tanta comida étnica en Miami como hoy en día. Pero no hubo tiempo para quejarme. Íbamos a Nueva York para encontrar nuestra familia.

Greyhound Bus #1, de un camino: Miami a la ciudad de Nueva York

25 de Febrero de 1957

En unas de las paradas que hizo la guagua, mi papa creyó que tenía tiempo para bajarse y comprar una soda y se quedó olvidado por el bus. Cuando nos dimos cuenta, mi mamá y yo le dijimos al conductor lo que pasó. Nos recomendó bajarnos en la próxima parada. El problema racial en el sur de los Estados Unidos estaba en su apogeo y nos sentamos en el salón de espera —para los blancos— y nos sacaron de el. Mi madre no entendía que ese lugar era reservado para las personas de la raza blanca y era prohibido a los negros. Nos dijo que debíamos sentarnos en el salón de los negros. Estábamos confundidos, enojados.

Esperamos una hora para la próxima guagua que traía a mi papa. Esa fue la pequeña y primera experiencia a nuestra llegada a los Estados Unidos. Al final, nos reunimos. Después llegamos a Nueva York donde mi Tío, hermano de mi mamá, nos esperaba.

Mi tío se llamaba Daniel Romero. Ya era ciudadano estadounidense viviendo en Nueva York. Nos dió la bienvenida con abrigos y una comida criolla—arroz con frijoles, plátanos fritos y carne—una *verdadera* comida. Nuestra familia estaba feliz de vernos y aún más porque habíamos llegado tarde. Tan solo llegamos que mi padre empezó a trabajar lavando platos y mi madre laboraba en una fábrica de vestidos—la misma profesión a que se dedicaba en Cuba también. Por mi parte conseguí trabajo en una fabrica de autos.

Cuando Fidel Castro tomó posición en Cuba, comencé mis estudios del inglés tomando clases de noche en Nueva York. Muchos de nosotros que laborábamos de día en fábricas o tiendas también estudiábamos de noche. Viendo películas en inglés también me ayudó poco a poco. Creo que hoy en día hay demasiadas oportunidades para que la gente hablen español y su urgencia de aprender el inglés ha bajado. Mientras trabajaba tanto, buscaba también seguir con mi arte en cada ocasión. Un profesor peruano me enseñaba por un tiempo. Pero la escena artística se había retrasado en general. Hasta la música también. Algunos entre los grandes músicos dominicanos y cubanos en aquellos días murieron, y de una forma murió también la música—nuestra música—con ellos. Hoy día veo que los ancianos no pueden bailar a la música moderna y tampoco pueden los jóvenes con las canciones antiguas.

Música y Arte

En los 1960s y 1970s la música tomó un papel muy importante en mi vida. Escuche Beny Moré, Sonora Matancera, Celia Cruz, Trío Matamoros, y Miguelito Valdez, Pérez Prado *(El Rey del Mambo)*,

Tito Puente *(El Rey)*, Boby Capó, Tito Rodríguez, Rafael Cortijo, y otros. Combiné mi pasión por el arte con mi amor por la música. Empecé a diseñar tapas de álbumes utilizando acuarelas y a veces al óleo. También me hice promotor de grupos y eventos musicales y de vez en cuando me substituía por el deejay (pinchadiscos). Una vez colaboré con el famoso promotor Don King. En esa época la música salsa llegó a ser muy popular. Originaba en la ciudad de Nueva York. La gente que hoy en día leen sobre la llegada de la salsa jamás conocerán lo que era vivirla. Estaba en el Bronx, en Queens, y en Harlem. El escenario arrancó a partir de medianoche y duraba hasta el amanecer; los hombres dando vueltas a las mujeres en las pistas, acogiendo los varios aspectos de las nuevas y viejas tradiciones. Nuestro mundo andaba por un ritmo particular en ese tiempo, tal como en la música. Era bien especial. Hubo una fusión de culturas, una verdadera mezcla. Hubo armonía.

Para desarrollar más mi negocio como artista y diseñador iba ofreciendo dibujar posters y anuncios para los negocios hispanos en el área como salones de belleza y hasta Goya. Creaba afiches, menús, catálogos, y revistas. Poco después llegué a tener empleados trabajando por mi. Preparé una revista de Santería y a la gente le gustó pero también algunos se sentían sorprendidos y algo asustados. Me decían "¡eso no se puede hacer!" En ese tiempo, la Santería todavía era una religión privada. Pero poco a poco me involucré más y más en ella. Aunque supe de la religión mientras vivía en Cuba, fue en Nueva York donde acogí un verdadero conocimiento. En el 25 de Diciembre del 1982 me inicié como Santero en un templo en East Elmhurst, Queens.

Greyhound Bus #2, de ida y vuelta: la ciudad de Nueva York a Nueva Jersey

1982

Mientras que iba involucrándome más en la Santería, asistía a muchas ceremonias y festivales y así conocí muchas personas. Conocí mi amiga Olga por primera vez en el Festival Patronas de Cuba en New Jersey. Ella vivía en Boston. Empecé a visitar Boston en los fines de semana y me paraba donde un hospedaje que ella arreglaba para los recién llegados a la ciudad llamado La Casa de la Caridad. Con tiempo me di cuenta de que hubo necesidad para una congregación de Santería en Boston. No habían botánicas ni lugares donde practicar la religión. Todavía la Santería tenía muy bajo perfil porque la gente tenían miedo. Algunos han confundido la Santería con el vudú, brujería, o los malos espíritus porque a veces sacrificamos animales en nuestras ceremonias. Por ejemplo a veces se sacrifica una gallina para marcar un momento significativo de la vida como un nacimiento, una boda, un entierro, o una iniciación en la religión. Sentí que me necesitaban en estas comunidades donde existía este temor por practicar lo que en realidad era bueno.

Creo que la tradición importa y hay que mantenerla. Los esclavos que hace siglos fueron trasladados a Cuba desde el África Occidental combinaron su fe original — la Yoruba — con el Catolicismo. Un santero es un cura pero también es psicólogo, curandero, mentor, y amigo. Como santero, ayudo a los que buscan evitar maldiciones y la mala suerte. Sugiero remedios herbales para los problemas cotidianos. Hay gente que toman el caldo de gallina o la aspirina para solucionar sus problemas. Para nosotros un té herbal o una breve ceremonia te consigue la misma meta.

Greyhound Bus #3, de un camino: Nueva York a Boston

1987

Después de haberme establecido con una vida completa en Nueva York, tomé la decisión de mudarme a Boston. Hasta ahora, muchos me preguntan, "¿Steve por qué se mudó a una nueva ciudad cuando tenía tantos amistades y familiares en Nueva York y además un negocio ya establecido?" Yo les respondo que me sedujo el encanto del carácter de Boston y su historia religiosa. Oraba a los santos y les preguntaba si ésta fuera buen idea. Con su respuesta decidí quedarme en Boston y construir mi propia congregación. Quise sacar la Santería de su closet. Me importaba disipar los mitos negativos y prejuicios que guardaban la gente sobre la religión.

En Septiembre del 2005 abrí una botánica en Jamaica Plain que se llamaba La Casa de Naturaleza. Hoy día se ubica en Brighton. Se puede decir que es el "Walgreens del Barrio." Yo me encargo de la tienda y sigo mi trabajo como Santero Obatala ordenado de la religión Yoruba. Siempre suena mi teléfono celular. A veces me llama una jovencita con problemas con su novio. O a veces es una pareja con dificultades de concebir un bebe. También me buscan los que están con "mal de ojo" o que están en problemas económicas. Hoy tengo más de dos mil personas en mi lista de contactos. Muchos me buscan antes de visitar a los médicos. Y la gente son de todas partes: Cuba, Puerto Rico, Brasil, Cabo Verde, y Cambridge también. Me encuentran por noticias transmitidas de una persona a otra. La Casa Obatala es el nombre del templo que mantengo en mi casa cerca de Dorchester Avenue. Allí tengo un salón de espera en el primer piso, un santuario en el segundo piso, y un cuarto ceremonial en el sótano.

También doy discursos en un "tour herbal" de Boston con la escuela de medicina de la Universidad de Boston en la facultad de medicina y el Boston Healing Landscape Project. Este proyecto examina las creencias culturales y religiosas de los inmigrantes nuevos a la ciudad. Creo que los alumnos allí me ven como un activista y un curandero, pero lo que mas quiero es ayudar a la gente. Muchos no se dan cuenta que los inmigrantes enfrentamos barreras con el idioma o errores culturales, y muchos no entienden como funciona el sistema de salud que actualmente tenemos en Estados Unidos. Cantidades ni tienen números de seguridad social. Yo no digo que un método es mejor que otro. Quiero servir como puente entre los inmigrantes y los médicos convencionales.

La única guagua que subo ahora es el numero 39 aquí en Boston. A veces me preguntan si me gustaría volverme a Cuba. Quizás algún día volveré a mi patria pero solo cuando se vaya el régimen comunista. Por ahora mi casa es la Casa de Obatala. De los muchos lecciones que he aprendido en mi vida, los que más valen son: amar la libertad y respetar América. Gracias a los dos, he podido disfrutar tanto aquí y servir a muchas personas.

Health and Wellness

THE POLIO WARD

Jean Sullivan

When I was growing up, we never swam in a pool in the summer. My mother forbade it, although she thought the ocean was okay because she felt that the saltwater was a purifier. She wasn't afraid of the water in public pools but rather the crowds who gathered there. She was afraid that someone in that crowd might have polio. That's how much everyone feared it. Every summer there would be a few cases of it. Two or three children in my neighborhood had polio and suffered paralysis. Polio, and the permanent paralysis it caused, changed life forever for so many people, including me. I never had polio, but it still changed my life.

For me, the high school years were wonderful. I was a good student and had a great bunch of friends. They were happy days with no peer pressure, and the drug of choice was ordinary cigarettes. If a girl smoked, she was considered "fast." A few boys smoked. There were house parties, football games, field hockey (which I loved), climbing Blue Hills on Sundays with my friends, and babysitting to earn my tuition.

I chose my classes carefully and took what was required to get into nursing school. I was accepted into three nursing programs but went with my first choice, the Peter Bent Brigham Hospital, which was a pioneer in the new medical field, as they had been first in early heart surgery, had performed the first kidney transplant, had the first dialysis machine in this country.

In 1952, I graduated high school and went off to Boston to become a "probie," which is what they called first year nursing students until they were capped. I formed a lasting bond with many wonderful people. The first six months were mostly intense study and classroom practice with a few trips to the wards under close supervision. Then on capping day we received our little white caps, which were made from a linen hankie. For some reason, unlike many other schools' caps, ours had no black stripe, a symbol of mourning for Florence Nightingale, who was the first real nurse.

In the next two and a half years, I left my youth behind and saw a path of life I had never known existed. Up to that point I had never really experienced life and illness up close. It was mentally and physically hard. People came to the Brigham from all over the world with their various maladies. Some were cured and went home while others died there. My classmates were very special people. In these stressful, demanding, and sleep-deprived times, we managed to put the wards behind us and go on to have many good times and loves.

In 1955, we were really prepared to go out into the world and face almost anything. The hospital had always been short-staffed, and the student nurses carried a heavy load of the work. We were mature beyond our years. It also happened that summer that we were to have the last but most devastating polio epidemic of our times.

After we finished training at Mary MacArthur Hospital in Wellesley, we nurses went to the Lemuel Shattuck Hospital in Jamaica Plain for additional training before the patients arrived. The team was made up of nurses, physical therapists, psychiatrists, nursing aides, technicians, and volunteers. We needed to become familiar with the mechanics of all the respirators, rocking beds, and a multitude of other equipment needed to keep these people alive. We all had our turn in the iron lung. We had to feel what it was like to depend entirely on others for every breath we took. We experienced the total dependence that the polio patients endured.

As soon as they were no longer contagious, the patients were transferred one by one from the various hospitals in the city. All adults, as well as children, stayed in the pediatric unit of the various Boston hospitals. The unit was staffed around the clock by our team. The patients that were totally dependent were kept in a large room called the solarium. I was assigned to the solarium, which housed six patients: Muriel, Ruth, Sol, Sumner, Hal, and Norman.

Jean in nursing uniform

Nurse-to-patient bonding was our top goal. We were all young and dedicated. We had thick skin, as one does at twenty years old. Our patients were grieving, frightened, and angry, but I knew that they were dependent on us. They needed constant physical therapy. They needed to be fed, washed, and scratched. Everything had to be done for them.

Rehabilitation was a day-to-day challenge for all of us. First, patients had to be weaned from the iron lung that breathed for them on to the rocking beds and chest respirators that allowed them to escape the confines the iron lung. When they came to us, some of them had already been weaned from the iron lung. Others we had to wean ourselves, which involved moving them from the iron lung to rocking beds that rocked the patients from head to toe to simulate exhaling and inhaling, helping their paralyzed diaphragms move. They rocked for so many hours a day and then moved to chest respirators, what we called chest pieces. Eventually, they only needed the iron lung at night.

As the days passed we all became more comfortable with each other. We were the patients' new family. Their own families came every day and were so faithful but started to show the strain. Even though spouses and children had hope for their loved ones, they knew that as time went on, their lives as they knew them were over. I watched one of our patients tell her husband not to visit anymore, not to bring the children. She told him to find a new life.

Most of the staff lived in the nurses' quarters. It was convenient, cheap, and helped stretch our meager salaries a little further. It cost us two dollars and fifty cents per week to live there, which was a good price as our salaries were two hundred fifty dollars a month. We often went back to the hospital after our shifts were over to take the patients to movie night, which was no easy task as they were on bed respirators. We had to push the beds and the respirators down the hall and into the service elevator to take them to the large conference room in the basement where we showed the movies. Everyone went to movie night, which was once a week, and it demanded a lot of staff. The patients really needed it; they needed a change of scenery. One of the orderlies, a young man from Maine, had an extensive record collection. Every night, he went back to play music and talk with some of the patients about music.

There was a cocktail hour every night for families and patients. Volunteer groups sometimes came to entertain, which usually provoked boos and jeers from the solarium crowd. Our patients had lost so much that they had become hardened in a way. They found it fun to torment entertainers. Ruth used to say, "Did you bring your peanuts to throw to the animals?" Ruth was what we called an "old polio," someone who had had the disease for two years already. She was very bitter. Needless to say, the entertainers didn't come too many times after that.

We soon joined the patients in playing private games such as taking bets on how many people would be killed on highway accidents on the holidays. One St. Patrick's Day, Ruth had the idea that all of the solarium patients should awaken with green hair. I was sworn to secrecy to find the green hair spray and go in at six in the morning to spray everyone's hair before the day staff arrived. The joke was on the staff, who came into the solarium to find that everyone's hair was green. After that it became a constant effort to top each prank.

Hal spent all of his time trying to devise a way of killing himself. He and Ruth were very close, even though their beds were across the room from each other. Try to imagine what your life would be like in their bodies.

I lasted a year and a half before feeling the need for a change. Ruth's husband died of a heart attack one night while visiting her. Our physical therapist, Brian, died in a plane crash. The boy from Maine, Timmy, had a nervous breakdown and tried to kill himself on the ward and was hospitalized. He had become too involved with the patients. No one saw how deeply involved he was.

After leaving, I kept in touch, especially with Ruth and Hal. Sol and Sumner went to a VA hospital. Norman transferred to a rehab center and eventually improved enough to be cared for at home. Muriel learned to enjoy being cared for and was the last to leave. Ruth and Hal lived only a few years more.

Thanks to two men, Sabin and Salk, we'll never have to relive that year again.

THE LOST YEARS

Cathy Gately

I was my father's favorite. When I was eight years old, sometimes Dad would take me to the bar with him. This was the forties and fathers did that then. Often Irish musicians played or step dancers performed. We just sat and talked with people; I might have had a Coke. We were at the House of the Murphy's in Jamaica Plain when the first person noticed that I was sick. I don't remember it coming on, but I had all the usual signs. I shook and twitched, and I got tongue-tied in the middle of a conversation. A woman told my dad, "You have a real sick daughter." He got upset and told her to sit back down and mind her business.

Soon after that my mother took me shopping at Jordan Marsh downtown. Going downtown was a big deal back then; you washed your face and got dressed up—it was a special occasion. I walked over to where a woman was looking at jewelry and my hand twitched, sending one of the earrings she was looking at flying across the aisle. My mother was so embarrassed and the other customer was none too happy.

A few days later, my mother was doing the washing while we slept. Apparently, I got up out of bed and scared her. She put a Mission Church prayer card in my hand, a picture of the Blessed Mother, and it folded up like an accordion in my grip. That day she made an appointment at Children's Hospital, where I was diagnosed with rheumatic fever and Saint Vitus's dance. The only known cure was plenty of bed rest and a ketogenic diet high in fats and low in carbohydrates. I was a string bean of misery anyway. Mother had no idea what they were talking about; she just knew I was really sick. There wasn't a room available at Children's Hospital, so we went to the House of the Good Samaritan; there was no room there, either. I was sent to the sanatorium way out in Sharon, Massachusetts, for eight months of bed rest.

A black car came to take my mother and me to the Sharon Sanatorium. It was raining hard. My mother cried all the way. The town is twenty-two miles from Boston, but the big highways didn't exist then, so the drive took hours. It seemed so far out in the sticks. The building had a big, long screened porch. We walked into the lobby to check in, and I began crying my eyes out. I thought my mother was mean for leaving me there. It was a lonesome, lonesome feeling.

There were about fifteen kids. We were all in a large room — boys on one side, girls on the other — with glass partitions between the beds. There was an office in the middle. Dr. Sieracki from Children's Hospital took care of me at the sanatorium. He came up once a week, with house doctors providing care the rest of the week. The nurses wore starched white uniforms, white shoes, and each wore a different white hat that indicated their rank. Nurse Terry was very

strict and had a temper; she had red hair and wore a pointy hat. Miss Lombardo's perfume was nauseating, but she was a big jolly woman and had a German accent, and we all loved her. I got a lot of attention from the nurses because I had curly, curly hair. I wore it like Shirley Temple and the nurses loved to brush it.

If it was a nice day, we were wheeled outside for the sunshine and fresh air and wheeled back inside in the evening. I got bad rashes from the rheumatic fever, so I had to take a lot of starch baths and had an enema every three days. It was purgatory. I was so itchy that I would take a hairbrush to bed with me—it's a wonder I'm not covered in scars from scratching.

Mother took the train out to Sharon every Sunday with my sister and brother. At ten and seven years old, Mary and Tommy were devils on wheels. Some Sundays Mary would get up at six in the morning and run out of the house so she wouldn't have to come to the hospital. They always caused a commotion when they visited. One time Tommy fell through the ice on the pond, and Mary dragged him out. Another time he climbed up the balcony to see me and fell off the porch. One time he was swinging on the wires and almost got electrocuted. They also liked to sneak into the kitchen and switch the patients' meals all around. Normally, my diet was like bunny food. After my brother and sister left, I had white powder biscuits with gravy or a plate of spaghetti until the nurses figured out what had happened and took it away. My brother and sister caused so much trouble that their visits made me feel worse. I was so nervous when they came that I told my mother not to bring them anymore. My father came to visit on Thursdays after he'd had a few cocktails at South Station. I was embarrassed; I didn't like that, but he made sure the doctors and nurses were taking care of me.

My best buddy was my Jewish doll. I don't know why it was called a Jewish doll; she had blond hair and a pretty little dress. One week, my mother couldn't come to visit, and I got so mad that I threw my doll at the window and broke the glass. Frankie Bowen, a boy I knew from Mission Hill, was also at the sanatorium. He had it worse than any of us; he was very, very sick. His father played organ at the church. When they came to see Frankie, his parents visited me, too. They talked to me the day I broke the glass and calmed me down.

Not long after that incident, I completely lost the use of my right hand. I didn't tell my mother that my right hand was paralyzed because I didn't want to worry her. She asked if I had sent my brother or sister a birthday card and I lied and said I had. Maybe the nurses told her I couldn't use my hand because she asked about it a lot.

I also could not walk. One time the other kids decided to run away. I encouraged them; I wanted to run away, too. When the time came, I tried to get out of bed but I couldn't move. My doll fell and made a loud noise so the nurses came running and caught the kids trying to escape. They all got spanked. The nurses called me the model patient and told them, "You should be more like Cathy!"

I became friendly with a girl there; her bed was next to mine and her name was Junebug. I think she died there. Of course no one told us that; she just wasn't there anymore and no one had seen her leave.

One day a new nurse put me in my starch bath and the water was too hot. She left me for a long time, and there was nothing I could do.

I couldn't move, and the faucets were so high that I couldn't have reached them anyway. I had to be rushed into a room with three or four towels; I was scalded and in bad shape. With occupational therapy, I slowly started to get my strength back. At first, I could only stand up for half an hour a day. I would be sent home when I was able to stand up for eight hours.

When I was able to get around a little better, I lived upstairs with the nurses for two months. I could hear them come in at night, their car lights flashing the walls as they pulled into the drive. They'd bring me bows for my hair and tell me about their dates.

In the eight months of my treatment, I learned to crochet and I read *Black Beauty*. The yodeling cowgirl Georgia Mae visited us at the Sanatorium. She wore a blue top and tight white pants. Later, after I was released, I listened to Georgia Mae on the radio from nine to nine-thirty every morning. She played the guitar and sang, "Get along towards the prairie, get along all day long, get along in the evening." When going off the air, Georgia Mae said, "Cowgirl, get outta here and get outta here fast!"

When the time came to leave the Sharon Sanatorium, I didn't want to go. I had cried the whole time I was there until the night I was to go home. After being away for so long, I felt like an outsider back home. It was a strange time. It took a while to get back in with the family, especially my brother and sister who had gotten along just fine without me. I thought they were so fresh. My sister took my toys and books and didn't talk to me.

I wasn't able to return to school for two years because I couldn't walk all the way up the hill, so I had a private tutor. I wasn't allowed to play, and I had to take naps every afternoon from noon to three o'clock. One time I was outside jumping rope with friends, and the neighbor called my mother. I was 10 or 11 years old before I finally went back to school. Even though I had only been in the sanatorium for eight months, it was years before my life returned to normal.

THE WHOOPING COUGH PARTY

Jo-Anne Palomba

When I was growing up in the North End, there were lots of kids my age and lots of birthday parties. I had been invited to a birthday party across the way, but whooping cough had broken out in the neighborhood. It was highly contagious, and the kids who had it weren't going to be able to go to the party. We got the news that the birthday girl had whooping cough, so only the children with whooping cough could attend. It was called the whooping cough party.

A SPORTING LIFE

Jack Chartoff

I started watching major league baseball as a kid in the early twenties. In the old days, we had two major league teams in Boston, the Red Sox in the American League and the Braves in the National League. As a result, there was a major league game played almost every day. Actually, back then I preferred going to the Braves games, because they were the better team. Wally Berger and Johnny Cooney were two of my favorite Braves. Berger was the home-run king and Cooney was a top pitcher.

I went to my first Red Sox game just after World War I, in 1919 or 1920. I was about seven or eight years old by then, and my friends and I went as part of a knothole gang. Back then you could get into a game and sit in the bleachers for a quarter, which was still a lot of money, but the bleachers were the best place to see the game. During those years, finding a seat was no problem. There were plenty of them available, so much so that the organization gave tickets to certain charities. You could buy tickets or apply to get tickets, and your ticket money went to the charity. I went to the games long into the

thirties when the price was as high as fifty cents. Back then, there were ten men for any woman at the games.

I was in high school when the stock market crashed and the Depression hit. At that time, I attended Boston Latin and in the summer, I liked to take the train to South Boston and go to the beach. From the train station, I could walk down L Street to the ocean and the L Street bathhouse, which is on Columbia Road. The bathhouse is a large building containing hundreds of lockers where you could undress before going to the beach. A privacy fence surrounded this section of the beach, so swimmers didn't have to wear a bathing suit. The section of the beach that I refer to was the men's side, where only men were allowed to enter.

L Street had a special appeal to me, as it was open all year, from nine in the morning to five at night, so I could go swimming any time of the year. That first summer I went to the beach I walked up and down to warm up after a swim. A man approached and asked, "Kid, what is your name?" I told him. He said, "Kid, you have a nice body. Would you like to develop it?" I discovered that this man's name was Dr. Feder. He was a Polish doctor in his forties, and a health enthusiast. He was tanned and had a beautiful body. He asked me to run up and down the beach a few times with him. He introduced me to a few other men who were his disciples, people who exercised with him on the beach.

From then on, every time I went to L Street, I would meet the doctor, who was a perpetual member there. I exercised with him to improve my strength and fitness, and then I would go for a swim. We swam all year in all weather. There was a whole group of us who would do these exercises, and he also encouraged us to go to the gym to work out there. After swimming in the ocean, I would go to the shower to wash up. One day, Dr. Feder told me not to take a shower until I got home or before I went to bed. He said the saltwater from the ocean was good for my health.

We called ourselves the L Street Brownies, and about once a month we would meet socially at someone's home. I was an L Street Brownie for almost forty years and I enjoyed it because of Dr. Feder. We swam even on the coldest days, about which we had an expression: "It will build you or kill you." Most people didn't exercise in any organized way in those days; Dr. Feder's philosophies for health were unusual.

I continued to swim with the L Street Brownies even as I attended Harvard. Back then, tuition at Harvard was four hundred dollars a year, which was a large sum of money. My father was a custom tailor, and because there was no work available during the Depression, he had to go to New York to get work. Even there he couldn't find much work. Though I was on the dean's list my freshman year, I dropped out of college because I couldn't pay the tuition. Instead, I got a job selling newspapers on the corner of Huntington Avenue and West Newton Street in front of Sawyer's Drugstore. I got ten dollars a week plus tips. I can't complain because it was worse for my younger sister. She was a top student in high school and wanted to attend college, but my mother told her, "I can't even afford to send your brother to college." She got a job at a drugstore for ten dollars a week, even though she was smarter than I was. Eventually, I went back to college and then to law school, and I got married—and all the while I kept swimming and watching baseball.

Wherever my wife and I went, we loved to swim. In Florida or on the Cape, I'd swim out for a hundred yards or a quarter of a mile, and then float on the water for a half hour or an hour and then come back. It was nothing to me to be in the water that long. The lifeguards didn't like it at first, but they got used to me when I did this. They warned me that they didn't want anyone else to get any ideas.

I continued to attend Red Sox games frequently. Over the years, I also got a reputation as a sports lover and was asked to sponsor a baseball player for the major leagues. The player I was to sponsor in 1954 was an All-American Hearst Newspaper selection catcher from Woburn High. His name was Joseph Castiglione. He wanted to play big-league baseball for the Red Sox, and he needed a sponsor. In those years, Major League Baseball had a rule that if a player signed a contract to play with a major league team and he took a signing bonus of more than five thousand dollars, he would have to stay on that team's roster. Because there was a limit to the total number of players who could be on any team, very few prospects were offered this bonus. As a result, few players of value signed up as they believed they were worth more than five thousand dollars. In fact, the only player who signed up that year for a large signing bonus was Bill Monboquette of Medford, who I understand later pitched a no-hitter.

The job of the sponsor was to act as the player's agent. The sponsor picked up all the bills and paid them out of his pocket, so you had to have big bucks to be a sponsor. The first thing I did when I became a sponsor was to write up Joe's capabilities and send them to all the major sports editors in the country, so they would write about him and promote him as an emerging talent. That was a major task.

The first call I got was from the manager of the Chicago White Sox. The team was going to play the New York Yankees in Yankee Stadium and wanted to see Joe work out for them before the game. I arranged for Joe and his older brother to take the train with me from South Station to Penn Station in New York. I also arranged for us to be put up in a nice hotel in Manhattan. The next morning he worked out with the White Sox. The Chicago manager liked the way Joe played. He hit a few long balls during practice. The manager asked me how much I wanted if they signed him. I said, "Fifty thousand dollars." The manager shrugged his shoulders and said in a laughing way, "Say, fellow, that's more than I am being paid as manager." They offered Joe five thousand dollars, the bonus limit. This was at a time when the salary for playing was practically nothing. If he didn't take the offer, he would have no contract.

Joe worked out with other teams, trying to get a better deal. He had the good fortune to work out in Miami with Satchel Paige, the legendary pitcher of the Negro Leagues. Joe said Paige was a regular guy and he enjoyed catching for him. Joe worked out for many major league teams who were interested in him, and I made the arrangements for him, but it was always the same old story—five thousand dollars or no contract. Joe had no choice. He signed as a bonus player with the Red Sox and took the five thousand dollars, which was his salary for the year. I believe he played for the minor league team in Lafayette, Indiana, for one year and then for another Red Sox minor league team the next year. By then, he'd had enough. He went home and became a regular citizen again. As for me, as a sponsor, it was a good experience. It cost me a few bucks, but I had a lot of fun, and I got a lot of fresh air.

LEARN, LEARN, LEARN

Raisa Karmiy

When I was in the eighth grade in the Soviet Union, I had a good friend named Emma. She was a very good student, especially in mathematics. Her mother was Russian but her father was Polish, a former colonel in the Polish army. He had been a prisoner in Siberia until 1945. Emma's family was afraid of everything because her father had opposed the communist regime in the past, and they always felt in danger. When Stalin passed away in 1953, school officials called a meeting. We stood in lines like soldiers and the principal told us that Stalin was dead. All of the teachers and many of the students cried.

Emma didn't cry. She knew from her father and mother who Stalin was. The next day our principal called Emma to her office. She asked Emma, "Why didn't you cry? The greatest leader of the proletariat is dead." Emma didn't answer. If it had been just one year before, this act would have put her family in jeopardy. They all could have gone to jail.

This is the reason I didn't like school at that time. The teachers never told students the truth about life. In my family, words about politics outdoors had always been forbidden. After I saw what happened to Emma, I realized why we had this rule. My eyes were opened. In the Soviet Union, you couldn't say what you really thought if you wanted to have an education, a job, and your own life. What was important to my parents was to educate their two daughters, to give us a chance at a job and a good life.

To do that, my father often pushed me. He pushed his family to adhere to his rules. Sometimes I didn't like the sounds that came from him. I was afraid of his loud voice, but he knew what was best for us. He had his own chair at the table, his own spoon. He had blue eyes, good skin. He was bald, smart, and practical. He had a terrible temper. He liked music, played the guitar, and could sing. He never asked me if I wanted to learn to play the piano. He brought the piano home and said, "You will play." I played for six years.

My father saved my life three times. When World War II began, my mother and I could not evacuate from the capital city of Kiev, and he saved us. He was a soldier, and my mother wasn't an active woman. Evacuation meant going to a train station that was packed with people in a panic. It was too dangerous. We waited in our apartment, waiting to be killed by German soldiers. One day, my father came and said to us, "What are you doing?" My mother said, "I can't evacuate." He said, "You will." And we did.

The second time, he saved my mother and me from the German fascists about a month later in Poltava. We needed to evacuate again, and again there was a panic. I was outside when I saw soldiers with

big cars. I was six years old. I saw him and yelled, "Papa! Papa!" He saw me and helped us, putting us on a train to Asia. He stayed with the army and we went to Uzbekistan.

The third time, he saved us from starvation near the end of the war. We were living in Uzbekistan. My mother and I had no food. My father was wounded in the leg and walked with crutches. In 1944 he came home to us. As a soldier he was able to find a job quickly and gave us his ration of food. He worked very, very hard, eating only a few dried apricots per day. He worked until he had money to buy food. He never ate any of the food he brought home. He gave it all to us. He was a strong man, a good father, and a good husband. I learned what family means from him. I was eleven years old.

When I was in ninth grade, I decided I wanted to be a doctor because I loved children and because I had a younger sister who was often ill. The Medical Institute of Lvov would be an open door for me when I finished tenth grade, but first I had to prove to myself that I could do the work. I went to an anatomical museum in the institute to see the cadavers. Many of my fellow students did the same. The cadavers didn't bother me.

This is when my father announced his rules. I was a beautiful girl. It was a difficult school. My father said, "No dancing. You have to come home at ten o'clock. Learn, learn, learn." Once I came home at midnight and he had locked the doors. No one let me in. I had to sleep at a neighbor's house. I learned what the rules were, what I couldn't do. My parents pushed me to do what I didn't want to do as a young girl. Now I can understand that they were right. Children don't grow up like mushrooms, with no one taking care of them.

I can't recall the moment when I began to think of myself as an adult, because the changes in life forced me to do what I had to for the family. When I was twenty years old, my father fell very ill. I was studying medicine. I had a small grant of money from the medical institute and took three courses, a full course load. My mother couldn't take a job, so I found a job as a nurse in the hospital ward for people with dangerous diseases. I worked three nights a week on twelve-hour shifts. At nine in the morning, right after work, I went back to the medical institute to study, and I didn't give up. On a student stipend and with money from my job, I had to support my mother, father, and sister, who was only eleven years old,.

I graduated and became a doctor, a pediatrician. I helped my family in this hard time. Children should pay parents back for all things that they did for us. I had a job that I loved, helping children to get well. I was a family doctor. I had 1,100 children in my area, ranging in age from seven days to fifteen years old. I had no car. I walked every day and in the winter I made twenty-five to thirty visits to children's homes to help them, in addition to my hours in the hospital. I found out later that doctors in the Soviet Union had the smallest salary of doctors anywhere in the world, but I never thought about those things. I was so happy to help poor and ill children.

I want to describe one day from my life when I felt under pressure in the children's hospital where I worked. At six o'clock at night, the ambulance delivered a small four-month-old girl. Her name was Nataly. She was in a very bad condition and had pneumonia. Her mother belonged to a religious sect whose members were forbidden to treat their children with medication or to meet with doctors.

The girl had been ill for about two weeks. The family doctor had told them that Nataly had a virus that would transform to pneumonia. Natalie needed medication — antibiotics—but they couldn't listen to the doctor because of their religion.

Nataly looked at me with big black eyes, full of suffering, as though she was asking me for help. I was fighting all night for Nataly's life, while her mother was crying all night. At eleven o'clock the next morning, Nataly passed away.

I told her mother, "You lost Nataly because you believed the people from the sect. Unfortunately, you didn't believe the doctors. If you had treated Nataly with medicine in time, she could be alive." She said, "You are right, but God gave me the baby child and God took my baby." The terrible story ended.

My life changed absolutely when I came to America. I was a pediatrician in the Ukrainian city of Lvov, a beautiful city with wonderful architecture, like a small Vienna. When I first came to America, I understood that I was a nothing, a big zero. I did not know the language. I did not have an American license. I couldn't speak to or communicate with American people. It was a terrible time for an educated person.

My father's lesson was still with me — "Learn, learn, learn." I went to Roxbury Community College and studied how to write and how to speak for three years. Now I can read and I speak with an accent. Sometimes I forget the correct word and substitute another word. This is not an easy time for me, but I was never looking for an easy life. That would not be interesting for me. My motto is "prove that if you are resolute you can survive an extreme situation." We should pay back our country and the American people. I like the words of John Kennedy: "Ask not what your country can do for you; ask what you can do for your country." That's why, after I came to this country, I volunteered in the Children's Hospital in Brighton for several years, and the Franciscan Children's Hospital in Brighton, where I worked with handicapped children. At the Farahat School in Boston, I worked as a tutor for four years teaching children writing, math, and music. I volunteered in the food pantry of the Boston Red Cross and the Home for Little Wanderers. I am happy to work in public service for the American people.

About the Authors

ANNA ADAMS ("Singing with the Saints," 33) was born in Jamaica Plain and has lived in Mission Hill since she was six years old. She was married for forty years and has six children, four girls and two boys. They all went to Mission Grammar and Mission Hill High School. She enjoys talking with friends, socializing, doing crossword puzzles, and being a senior citizen.

MARYALICE BELLEW ("Surviving in Close Quarters," 42; "The Wicker Rocking Chair," 47) was born in 1933 in Boston's Hyde Park area. She attended the Boston public schools. Maryalice still lives in the Boston area in the family home with her two children. She is an active member of the Hyde Park Art Association.

JACK CHARTOFF ("A Sporting Life," 237) was born in Roxbury in November 1912. He attended the Phillip Brooks Grammar School, Boston Latin High School, Harvard College, and Northeastern Law School. He has been a member of the bar since 1941 and was a legal advisor to the Postal Union. He was a member of the Young Democratic League and wrote speeches for politicians to whom he was assigned. He was a member of the L Street Brownies for forty years and swam in the ocean year-round. He was married for over forty years until his wife, Sarah, passed away. His daughter lives in Maine.

JOHN CLIFFORD ("Breadwinning," 15) was born July 31, 1926, in Saint Francis DeSales Parish near Dudley Street in Roxbury. He moved to Mission Hill in August 1928 when he was two years old. He has lived there for more than eighty years. In 1943, he graduated from Mission Church High School. He earned his bachelor's degree in business administration at Boston University, and his master's degree in education from the State College at Boston. John worked as a teacher in the Boston Public Schools, an administrator with the State Department of Education, and a guidance counselor in the Waltham Public Schools for a total of thirty-nine years.

MARY CLIFFORD ("Ellie's Coffee and Donut Shop," 3) was born in 1933 in the Lying In Hospital in Mission Hill. She spent her whole life in Mission Hill. She owned the Ellie's Coffee and Donut Shop at 1516 Tremont Street from 1962 to 1976. Mary passed away in 2010, and is survived by a younger sister, Cathy Gately, two nieces, and a beloved nephew Jimmy, who she helped care for.

GAIL COWGILL ("My Journey to Jamaica Plain," 137) was born and brought up in Lowell. She graduated from Lowell High School in 1960. She now lives in her own condo in Jamaica Plain, where she spends most of her time gardening. Twelve years ago, Gail took master gardening classes through BNAN (Boston Natural Areas Network) and is now a Master Gardener. "Thanks to Mayor Menino's support for community gardens, I can grow my own veggies. Gardening is great exercise and wonderful for my health. Thank you, Mayor Menino!"

KATHLEEN MCKINLEY TAYLOR DASH ("The Big Four and Esmeralda: A Sisterhood," 55) was born in Boston on February 8, 1937. Her adoptive parents, Lillian and Edward Taylor, emigrated from Jamaica, British West Indies, in 1917 and 1919, respectively. After graduating from Girls' Latin and Boston Clerical schools, she entered federal government service where she worked for forty-one years. A widow for the past twenty-four years, Kathleen has one son, Randall. Her volunteer experiences include working in the research department at the Hebrew Rehabilitation Center. "I truly enjoyed this writing experience! Thank you to the City of Boston and Grub Street for this opportunity."

OLGA DUMMOTT ("Working for Justice," 95) has been involved in countless community organizations in Boston since 1948. Her many roles include founder of La Casa de la Caridad, founder of the first Cuban community in Roxbury, former vice president of ABCD (Action Bureau for Community Development), representative of Roxbury North APAC (Action Planning Advisory Committee), and coordinator for elderly services in Jamaica Plain. She is the recipient of numerous awards and commendations for her civic contributions, including most recently a 2009 Latina leadership award from the League of United Latin American Citizens (LULAC). She has one daughter, two grandchildren, fourteen great-grandchildren, and one great-great-grandchild.

Desde 1948, OLGA DUMMOTT ("Embajadora a los Mayores," 95) se ha involucrado en muchas organizaciones comunitarias. Sus contribuciones incluyen: fundadora de la Casa de Caridad, la primera comunidad cubana en Roxbury, vise-presidente de La ABCD, la representada de Roxbury APAC, la coordinador de servicios para la gente mayor en Jamaica Plain. Olga ha recibido varias adjudicaciones debidas a su trabajo en la comunidad incluso la adjudicación de 2009 de LULAC(League of United Latin American Citizens). Ella tiene una hija, dos nietos, catorce bisnietos y uno bis-bisnieto.

MARGARET DUNN ("Big Changes," 69) was born in 1916 in North Wilmington. After attending schools in Springfield and Connecticut, she lived in Hyde Park and worked in Boston at the State House. For thirty-eight years, she worked at the Gillette Company in the advertising department. She enjoys playing piano, dancing, gardening, painting, writing poems, sewing, and all handiwork.

GLADYS CHUTE FACEY ("Miss Facey," 130) was born in Somerville on March 20, 1922. With her husband, William, she moved into Jamaica Plain's Bromley Heath Apartments in 1956 and raised their two children and grandchildren. Known as Miss Facey or the Lady in Purple, Gladys babysat two generations of children too numerous to count throughout Bromley Heath. As a senior, she was very active in Boston's elder affairs and activities. As she said, "You're never too old to learn something new." Gladys passed away September 18, 2010.

JOAN O'NEILL FLYNN ("A Portrait of Nana Doherty," 174) was born in Boston in December 1930. She grew up in Roxbury and graduated from high school in Jamaica Plain. She and her husband, Joe, met at a teen dance at the Norfolk House in Eliot Square in 1947 and were married at Saint Mark's Church in Dorchester in 1952. They lived in a Brighton housing development and moved to Hyde Park with their five children in 1971. They now have eight grandchildren and three great-grandchildren. Joan enjoys sports, sewing, knitting, and gardening, but her favorite thing to do is visit Walt Disney World. Joan and Joe have been happily married for fifty-seven years and have spent all of their years in Boston.

GLORIA GANNO ("Urban Renewal: My Two Lost Neighborhoods," 109) is a lifelong resident of Boston and grew up in the South End. She has great memories and knowledge about what it was like to live in the inner city during the forties and fifties. She has regaled her three children with interesting, humorous, and sometimes bizarre stories about her old city neighborhood, and they've always asked for more. When her two grandchildren are old enough, she plans to do the same for them, hopefully with similar results. After retiring at age sixty-two, she used her strong interest in history to begin a new career writing about Boston's historic events.

CATHY GATELY ("The Lost Years," 229) has lived in Mission Hill for seventy-three years. She went to school at Mission High and was married by Father McDonough, the charismatic healing priest. Cathy is the mother of three children, two girls and one boy. She retired from the Brookline school system.

ROBERT F. HANNAN ("Locked in a Cemetery," 197) has lived in the same home on Ayles Road in Hyde Park since returning from a honeymoon trip to Yellowstone National Park in July 1959. His bride, Nancy (Hughes) Hannan, a lifelong Hyde Park resident, was with him until her passing in February 2008. It was through her long-time presidency of the Hyde Park Historical Society that his interest in local history developed. Bob grew up near Tufts College in Medford. He attended Northeastern University for the cooperative work-study course in English and journalism. Subsequently, he worked for the old *Boston Herald* in general assignment, then as an assistant at the State House, then as a city hall reporter. Later he was chief of research for the Boston City Council, retiring in 1996.

BARBARA P. HOPWOOD ("The Early Days of Motherhood," 63) was born to a family of twelve in East Bridgewater in 1932. She raised six children and has thirteen grandchildren and three great-grandchildren. Barbara moved to Hyde Park in 1988. She is the president of Jolly Aces, a past trustee of her condo association, and sits on the Advisory Council for the City of Boston. Barbara is an avid ballroom dancer and roller-skater.

FRANCESCA (GALANTE) JOHNNENE ("Looking Back on Busing," 117) was born in Readville to an American-born father and an Italian-born mother. She is the eldest of three children and was educated at Catholic schools. Her career has been devoted to the service of the people of Boston for more than thirty-seven years. Most recently she was the director of Boston's Retired Senior Volunteer Program (RSVP), a part of the Commission on Affairs of the Elderly, for eighteen years. Fran created the *Boston Seniors Count* radio show on Allston Brighton Free Radio (1630 AM) and on WJIB (740 AM), and moderated the *Boston Seniors Count* TV show on BNN. Fran is also a member of the Professional Women's Club of Boston and has twice served as its president.

ANITA JONES ("Keeping Busy at the Pharmacy," 8) was born in Roxbury in 1931. She has lived in Dorchester since 1955. She has four children, one of whom is still living, seven grandchildren, and seven great-grandchildren. Her husband of forty-one years died in 1993. She keeps herself busy by doing a lot of volunteer work. Most recently, she has helped to inform senior citizens of the services available to them and helped them fill out forms to describe their needs and obtain city services.

RAISA KARMIY ("Learn, Learn, Learn," 243) was born in 1935 in Kiev, the capital city of Ukraine. During World War II, she was evacuated several times to evade the fleeing German army. She faced starvation and often feared for her life. This has given her great compassion for children who are sick or suffer wartime trauma. She graduated from the Medical Institute of Lvov and worked for thirty-two years as a pediatrician in that same area. She moved to Boston in 1992. She lives in Mission Park, a community-run, subsidized housing development in Mission Hill with her husband of fifty years. She has one son and she describes her two grandsons as smart, active, and energetic Americans.

GWENDOLYN KEITH ("Some Dreams Do Come True," 125) was born June 14, 1916, at Newton-Wellesley Hospital to Stella and John Myers. She went to Newton schools and graduated in 1935. Although she dreamed of being a nurse, she went to work taking care of babies. She married Willie Keith on December 1, 1940. She fulfilled her dream of becoming a nurse at age fifty-five.

ANN LABBE ("The Aunt Who Spoiled Me," 153) grew up in the Mission Hill projects from 1946 to 1967, though she supposes today it would be called a nine-unit condo. Ann was the youngest of four. She married Robert P. Labbe in 1967, and they moved to Jamaica Plain in 1971. They were married for thirty-seven years and had three children, two daughters and a son, and five beautiful grandchildren. "To my children and my grandchildren, my saying in life is: 'I'm leaving memories, not money,' and I think I'm doing a damn good job of it."

JULIA MARTIN ("Thank You, Mother Atkinson," 160) was born in Wareham in 1929 and moved to Jamaica Plain in 1954. She has been a community activist since her husband's death in 1972. Her activism was recognized by Boston's MDC when they named a building after her, the Julia Martin House. She has five children, three of whom are still living, forty-two grandchildren, fifty-five great-grandchildren, and two great-great-grandchildren.

ALTA KILTON MCDONALD ("Maine Course," 49) was born in 1934 in Machiasport, Maine. She is a graduate of the University of Maine in Orono. After receiving her master's degree in social work from the University of Denver in 1959, she moved to the Boston area where she had a dual career track as a social worker and a college professor. She has two children and two grandchildren. Since retiring, she volunteers for Generations, Inc., as a site coordinator in an after-school literacy program at St. Stephen's Church in Boston's South End. She is a founding member of the Jamaica Plain Common Security Club and a member of the advisory board of the Jamaica Plain Forum. Alta enjoys creating original jewelry with semiprecious stones and found materials under the label of Alta Rocks.

ELSA NIN ("'Sewing' the Seeds of a Better Life," 143) was born in Barahona, Dominican Republic in 1936. She came to Boston in 1967. She became an American citizen in the seventies. Elsa worked for many years in the interior design industry. She has four children, seven grandchildren, and two great-grandchildren.

ELSA NIN ("'Sembrando' las Semillas de una Vida Mejor," 143) nació en Barahona, la Republica Dominicana en 1936. Vino a Boston en 1967. Se hizo ciudadana en el 1970. Elsa trabajaba por muchos años en la industria de diseño interior. Tiene cuatro hijos, siete nietos y dos bisnietos. La Sra. Nin vive en Jamaica Plain.

JO-ANNE PALOMBA ("The First Date," 37; "The Whooping Cough Party," 236) was born in the North End, the oldest of three girls. Her family moved to Jamaica Plain when she was fourteen. She attended Boston public schools, the Paul Revere & Eliot Elementary schools, Michelangelo Junior High, Girls' High School, and Boston Clerical School. She has a wonderful husband, Remo, with whom she has shared fifty-one years of marriage. They have two lovely daughters, Susan and Cheryl, four granddaughters, and one great-granddaughter.

REMO PALOMBA ("Rolling with the Punches," 75) was born on February 28, 1937, in the North End of Boston. He married his nursery school sweetheart in 1958. The couple raised their two wonderful daughters in Jamaica Plain. Remo worked as an upholsterer and laborer for forty years and is now semi-retired, working a few hours a day at St. Thomas Aquinas, the church where he was married.

ALICE PALUMBO (*"Cammenare Diretta* [Walk a Straight Line]," 183) was born in 1923 in the Readville section of Hyde Park to first-generation Italian immigrants. She is one of eleven children, five boys and the youngest of six girls. She married her childhood sweetheart in 1949 after she got out of the marines. She has two children. She is the oldest living charter member of the American Legion Auxiliary Post 458. Alice volunteers at the Brookline Harvard Vanguard where she meets with seniors and encourages them to be active. She is on call with the Retired Senior Volunteer Program (RSVP).

THERESA PARKS ("Saving Mission Hill," 89) was born in Jamaica Plain, the second daughter of wonderful parents. Her family moved to the Mission Hill Project in the forties and she has lived in Mission Hill ever since. "Our neighbors were like family to us growing up. It was a very loving and caring environment." She and her sister Anna went to Catholic schools in the neighborhood. She met her husband Bob when he was at Boston College. They had four children and three grandchildren. She and Bob were involved with many neighborhood groups that existed to keep Mission Hill a place where folks could raise their families and work. Her husband died in 2000, and a community building at Mission Park was named after them. She hopes the work they did to get Mission Park built will be their legacy to Mission Hill, to keep affordable housing available to everyone.

ESTEBAN "STEVE" QUINTANA III ("Every Time I Ride the Greyhound Bus, My Life Changes," 204) was born in Havana, Cuba, in 1939 and moved to New York City at the age of sixteen. For thirty years, Steve worked as a graphic studio artist in Brooklyn, until 1987 when he moved to Boston. He has two daughters, Caridad and Rejina, and one son, Esteban Quintana IV. Currently, Steve works as an ordained Obatala Priest of the Yoruba Religion and manages the House of Mother Nature, a store in Brighton. He lives in Jamaica Plain.

ESTEBÁN QUINTANA III ("Cada Vez Que Monto el Autobús de Greyhound, Mi Vida Cambia," 204) nació en La Habana, Cuba en 1939 y él se movió a la ciudad de Nueva York a la edad de dieciséis. Durante treinta años, Steve ha trabajado como artista gráfico en el estudio de Brooklyn, hasta 1987, cuando se trasladó a Boston. Tiene dos hijas, Caridad y Rejina, y un hijo, Estebán Quintana IV. Actualmente, Steve trabaja como Obatala ordenado sacerdote de la religión yoruba y maneja La Casa de la Madre Naturaleza, una tienda en Brighton. Él vive en Jamaica Plain.

HECTOR RIVERA ("The Trips of My Life," 189) originally came to Boston on a two-week vacation during the summer of 1964. He became enamored by the history, culture, and beauty of Boston, and decided to stay. Hector also served in the United States Army and has spent time in Kentucky, New York, and Miami. While he frequently visits Puerto Rico, where he has published poetry in Spanish, Hector calls Boston his home. He works as a medical translator in city hospitals.

HÉCTOR RIVERA ("Los Viajes de Mi Vida," 189) originalmente llegó a Boston en un período de dos semanas de vacaciones durante el verano de 1964. Se convirtió en enamorado de la historia, la cultura y la belleza de Boston, y decidió quedarse. Héctor también sirvió en el Ejército de los Estados Unidos y ha pasado tiempo en Kentucky, Nueva York y Miami. Aunque Héctor visita Puerto Rico regularmente, donde ha publicado poesía en español, el dice que Boston es su hogar. Trabaja como traductor médico en hospitales de la ciudad.

RITA ROGERS ("No Easy Job," 21) has eleven children, nine of whom are still living. She has fifty-three grandchildren, countless great-grandchildren, and six great-great-grandchildren—so far. She was born in Boston in 1928 and grew up in Roxbury. She has lived in Jamaica Plain for four years. After she finished raising her children and grandchildren, she worked for ten years in the Henry Buckner School in Cambridge where she helped raise yet another generation of children.

BLANCHE SABINA ("Tough Choices," 26) was born in 1927 in Hyde Park, the daughter of Polish immigrants. She worked in automation for over forty-five years while she raised a family of four children. Blanche was one of the working mothers who had mothers' hours. She was married to Frank Sabina for fifty-nine years. Blanche is active in Hyde Park senior groups.

JEAN SULLIVAN ("The Polio Ward," 223) was born in 1934 in Canton where she grew up in a family of second-generation Italians. She has lived in Jamaica Plain for nearly forty years. She has been married thirty-six years to her beloved husband, Larry Sullivan. She has been a member of the Jamaica Plain Tuesday Club for thirty years and is a past president. This 120-year-old philanthropic club was started by the Brahmin women of Jamaica Plain in the 1890s and is the oldest women's club in Massachusetts. The club meets in the Loring-Greenough House, a Colonial-era home that has been preserved.

JOHN VACCARO ("Good Family, Good Friends," 80) was born in 1925 and entered the service in 1943, when he was seventeen years old. He was discharged in 1946 and went to work on the railroad in Readville just like his father and grandfather. He married Grace in 1950 and they have been together ever since. They have three children and started a business called Marascio's Market. John has been a friend to his customers for more than fifty years. So far, he has five grandchildren, and one great-grandchild.

GLORIA WRIGHT ("Baseball, an Autograph book, Aunt Clara, Einstein, and Me," 167) was born April 11, 1933, in Culpepper, Virginia, the third of five children born to Lloyd and Frances Wormley. She attended Hampton Institute with money she'd earned from providing childcare and cooking services from her youth. In 1954, she made an independent move to Massachusetts and subsequently married John Wright in 1957 in New Bedford. Gloria worked as a recovery room nurse at New England Deaconess Hospital, then became an entrepreneur and opened a convenience store at 1070 Tremont Street, which she ran for over twenty-five years until retiring in 1995. Gloria has lived in Mission Hill for more than forty years since she and her youngest brother Harvey moved there following her divorce.

For Further Reading

BOOKS ABOUT WRITING MEMOIR

Abercrombie, Barbara. *Courage and Craft: Writing Your Life into Story.*
Novato, CA: New World Library, 2007.

Barrington, Judith. *Writing the Memoir: From Truth to Art.* Portland,
OR: The Eighth Mountain Press, 2002.

Boga, Steve. *How to Write Your Life Stories: Memoirs That People Want
to Read.* Xlibris Corporation, 2009.

Goldberg, Natalie. *Old Friend from Far Away: The Practice of Writing
Memoir.* New York: Free Press, 2008.

Ledoux, Denis. *Turning Memories into Memoirs: A Handbook for
Writing Lifestories.* Lisbon Falls, ME: Soleil Press, 2005.

Lippincott, Sharon M. *The Heart and Craft of Lifestory Writing: How
to Transform Memories into Meaningful Stories.* Pittsburgh, PA:
Lighthouse Point Press, 2007.

Norton, Lisa Dale. *Shimmering Images: A Handy Little Guide to
Writing Memoir.* New York: St. Martin's Griffin, 2008.

Silverman, Sue William. *Fearless Confessions: A Writer's Guide to
Memoir.* Athens, GA: University of Georgia Press, 2009.

Spence, Linda. *Legacy: A Step-by-Step Guide to Writing Personal
History.* Athens, GA: Swallow Press/Ohio University Press, 1997.

Styne, Marlys Marshall. *Seniorwriting: A Brief Guide for Seniors Who
Want to Write.* West Conshohocken, PA: Infinity Publishing, 2007.

BOOKS ABOUT HYDE PARK, MISSION HILL, AND JAMAICA PLAIN

Hannan, Nancy H. *A Compendium of Hyde Park History*. Hyde Park, MA: Albert House Publishers, 1988.

Olmsted, Frederick Law. *Civilizing American Cities: Writings on City Landscapes*. Cambridge, MA: Da Capo Press, 1997.

Putnam, Harold. *Yankee Journal: A Memoir of Public Service*. Kearney, NE: Morris Publishing, 1998.

Roboff, Sari. *Hyde Park* (Boston 200 Neighborhood History Series). Boston: The Corporation, 1976.

Roboff, Sari. *Mission Hill* (Boston 200 Neighborhood History Series). Boston: The Corporation, 1976.

Sammarco, Anthony Mitchell. *Forest Hills Cemetery*. Mount Pleasant, SC: Arcadia, 2009.

Sammarco, Anthony Mitchell. *Hyde Park*. Dover, NH: Arcadia, 1996.

Sammarco, Anthony Mitchell. *Images of America: Jamaica Plain*. Mount Pleasant, SC: Arcadia, 2004.

Sammarco, Anthony Mitchell. *Jamaica Plain: Then and Now*. Mount Pleasant, SC: Arcadia, 2003.

Von Hoffman, Alexander. *Local Attachments: The Making of an American Urban Neighborhood, 1850 to 1920*. Baltimore: Johns Hopkins University Press, 1996.